Miracles of a Misunderstood Woman

by Jimmy Jack

Copyright © 2018 by Jimmy Jack

www.jimmyjackny.com

ISBN# 978-1717320476

No part of this publication may be reproduced, stored in a retrievable system, or transmitted in any form or by any means, electronic or mechanical, including photocopy, recording, or any other information storage and retrieval system without prior written permission of the author, publisher, Jimmy Jack Ministries nor be otherwise circulated in any form of binding or cover other than that in which it is published and without a similar condition being imposed or subsequent purchaser.

All quotes used by permission.

Unless otherwise indicated, scripture quotations are from the Holy Bible, New King James, copyright © 1996, 2004, 2007. Used by permission of Tyndale House Publishers Inc., Carol Stream, Illinois 60188.

ENDORSEMENTS

Jimmy Jack brings alive the story of the biblical Hanna. The miracle of a broken heart healed by God's power will inspire, instruct, and bring hope to the reader male as well female. I have gained insights from reading this book. Hanna's story is both timely and timeless. It mirrors many of the struggles anyone of us may have which can be miraculously healed.
Rev. Don Wilkerson, Co-Founder of Teen Challenge

In a day of agnosticism and disbelief in the supernatural, Jimmy Jack makes a powerful case for God who intervenes into our lives! Don't miss reading *Miracles of a Misunderstood Woman*.
Jim Cymbala, Senior Pastor of The Brooklyn Tabernacle

Jimmy Jack's new book *Miracles of a Misunderstood Woman* will inspire you and give you a new picture of the depth of God's grace.
Carol Cymbala, The Brooklyn Tabernacle Choir Director

Miracles of a Misunderstood Woman is a message of hope and healing to those who have been deeply wounded and empty. Jimmy Jack dissects the soul of Hannah and captures her miracle transformation and the fulfillment of her dreams through his personal insight working with broken people over the past 30 years. It's a book you will read twice.
Mark Batterson,
Author and New York Times best-selling author of The Circle Maker

Everything in life does not go exactly the way we thought it would. Our unfulfilled expectations have the potential of turning into disappointment, depression and despair. In Miracles of a Misunderstood Woman, we see Hannah as she takes her broken heart and wounded soul, and gives it to the only One who can mend them. Jimmy Jack shares a timeless message of healing and restoration for all who are looking for hope.
Rose Marie Bravo,
Former CEO of Burberry, President of Saks Fifth Avenue

Thank you for the privilege to read Miracles of a Misunderstood Woman. The book is awesome and worth reading. It ministered to me and it will do its intended work as programmed by the Lord. .
Dr. Saji Abraham,
Clinical Professor Cardiology, N.Y. University Medical Center

Miracles of a Misunderstood Woman

Through Hannah's story, Jimmy Jack weaves a story of loss and grief and hope and an unexpected story that became larger than the original dream. This is a book to inspire all those who have lived with buried hopes and dreams to continue to cling to God and release the dreams and brokenness to a gracious God who is still turning mourning into dancing and writing miraculous stories through the lives of His children.
Dr. Carol Taylor, President of Evangel University

I was there the first time Pastor Jimmy preached about Hannah. I was immediately struck by the power of the message and the need for him to share it. We have witnessed Pastor Jimmy labor for hours in prayer, research and manuscript preparation for this book. It is more than a book about a women that was misunderstood. Miracles of a Misunderstood Woman is a message of hope and promise for anyone who thinks their brokenness is beyond the reach of God's grace.
Bernie & Cathy Gillott, Evangelism Director, Global Teen Challenge

Dedicated to the Gospel of Jesus Christ to transform lives, Jimmy Jack captures through his insight on the life of Hannah, the tenacity of anyone who would dare to believe God and pray; no matter what the situation! His message will encourage and inspire you in your own journey. .
Michael Durso, Senior Pastor of Christ Tabernacle

Jimmy Jack has masterfully unpacked the life of one of the most beloved and relatable characters in the Bible. Anyone who has experienced a long season of heartache and pain will be thoroughly ministered to as you lose yourself in every spirit filled line.
Maria Durso, Author and Pastor of Christ Tabernacle

There is no better approach to Bible study than to take a story, retell it and try to bring it to life. Jimmy Jack has hit the mark. You will know you have walked in Hannah's sandals in the time she lived. This story of redemption, *Miracles of a Misunderstood Woman*, will give hope to any reader dealing with emotional trauma.
Ann Floyd, former associate editor of Pentecostal Evangel

Don't be misled…this book isn't just for women. In *Miracles of a Misunderstood Woman*, Jimmy Jack leads us through a journey that one woman bravely faced. He shows the steps she took to overcome and gain victory over bitterness and how you can allow God to exterminate strongholds that are keeping you miserable and turn your tragedy into triumph.
Kathy Arnett, Director of Development, Northpoint Bible College

Miracles of a Misunderstood Woman

Table of Contents

DEDICATION vii

ACKNOWLEDGMENTS ix

INTRODUCTION 1

Chapter 1 – MISSION 3

Chapter 2 – MARRIED 15

Chapter 3 – MARKED 23

Chapter 4 – MISERABLE 33

Chapter 5 – MISUNDERSTOOD 47

Chapter 6 – MARRED 63

Chapter 7 – MIRACLES 75

          EXAMINED HER SOUL 77

          EXTREME PRAYER 85

          EXTERMINATE THE STRONGHOLDS 95

          EXPECT YOUR MIRACLE 111

          ENDNOTES 127

DEDICATION

I dedicate this book to my beautiful, faithful wife, **Miriam.**

When I first met you right out of high school, we danced the nights away in the world. We never realized that seven years later we would be dancing and rejoicing in God's divine destiny for our lives.

In every building project, outreach and the many ministries we established, your deep insight and fervent prayer strengthened my spirit from the very beginning and even until today. Some of my fondest memories are when we moved to Springfield, Missouri and we enrolled into Central Bible College (CBC) for ministry training in our early years. You were such an encouragement especially studying together and memorizing scriptures for our classes we took together. Thank you for being my greatest fan when I played basketball for CBC weather we won or lost the games you always saw me as a winner..

The years you have expereinced providing healing and hearing the cries of broken hearts through our ministries have produced in you a treasury of wisdom and understanding. Your insights and godly discernment that you have shared with the countless women, couples and families has brought restoration and redemption into multitudes of lives. I am so grateful for your insights that you have given to me as in writing this book.

The mission and journey we have been on for the past 25 years, restoring broken lives through the love of God, have been exciting, challenging and so rewarding. Over the years, we have been privileged to share in the "new birth" of hundreds of spiritual children through our Teen Challenge ministries and Freedom Chapel International Worship Center. But God has truly blessed us with the three most beautiful and gifted, God-fearing children, David, Dionniza and Dominique. Miriam, you lovingly and tirelessly poured your life into them in the midst of the great challenges and burdens that we faced in the many missions that God entrusted to us.

Thank you for your love, your patience, your encouragement, your dedication and your full support. You have blessed me with the freedom over the past three years of study, the many days of travel, and the countless hours of writing required to complete this book.
Bless you, my Love.

You are my Woman of Miracles!

ACKNOWLEDGMENTS

I am deeply thankful for **Bernie and Cathy Gillott** for their hours of dedication in editing *Miracles of a Misunderstood Woman* with me. I am so privileged to have had the expertise and the genius of this duo with their years of experience, not only in their writing and editing skills, but their decades of studying God's Word and working with broken people.

As Global Evangelism Coordinators, they are *hands on* in the mission field, serving precious, needy people around the world in over 50 countries, in their work with Global Teen Challenge. Through over 30 years of ministry with Teen Challenge, their compassion and ministry to the hurting have given them a depth of understanding of the human soul that has enhanced our team with inspiring insight in editing and writing this book.

Bernie and Cathy have established Teen Challenge Choirs all over the world and minister with me throughout New York City and overseas at our Rock the Block Outreaches and leadership conferences. Bernie is not only a skilled editor but also a gifted preacher, musician, video technician and even raps in over 10 languages.

The times we spent together over the past three years have been rich, deep, challenging and fun. Their overflowing joy and great sense of humor were especially needed through the long hours of editing.

From the bottom of my heart, I thank you for your labor of love.

To My Ministry Leadership Team

My heartfelt thanks go to my leadership at Teen Challenge and Freedom Chapel. Their faithful encouragement, diligence and spontaneous cooperation secured and upheld all the ministries. This freed me up and allowed me to take the quality time needed to study and write this book.

To **Willie Ramos**, the Executive Director of Long Island Teen Challenge, I want to personally thank you for not only holding the fort, but for your encouragement over the years that lightened the many burdens. Your servant leadership made it possible for me to dedicate the time needed to focus on the manuscript and complete this project.

A special acknowledgment goes to **Cathy Smith**, my lead administrator at Freedom Chapel. Your faithfulness, outstanding leadership and wisdom to oversee the church office in my time of absence have blessed and inspired me to fulfill this vision God gave me for this book.

Finally, thank you to **Jeremy David**, who assisted me in the early stages, gathering the needed study resources and developing the preliminary outline of the manuscript.

To all of you, I leave this expression of gratitude: "We give thanks to God always for you all, making mention of you in our prayers, remembering without ceasing your care work of faith, labor of love, and patience of hope in our Lord Jesus Christ in the sight of our God and Father" (1 Thessalonians 1:2, 3).

Introduction

Throughout my life and years of ministry, I have been touched by the obedience and sacrificial love of great women of God.

Four of the key role models in my life were women. First, my mother and sister, Dianne, whose miraculous transformation showed me the path to saving grace. At Teen Challenge, directors Sandy Segrest and Yolanda Planas Cartegna were shining examples of what it meant to model the life of Christ in the real world.

As I trained for the ministry, I was incredibly inspired by their dedication and passion. As I observed their lives and faith, I was challenged to go deeper with God and discover my life's mission.

Several years ago, I prepared a sermon on Hannah, the mother of Samuel, a great Old Testament prophet. I was inspired by her traumatic, yet triumphal journey.

I have realized that people with great vision and purpose are often misunderstood. Their dreams are trampled on by doubt, discouragement and despair. Shattered dreams are not a condition exclusive to Israel 1,000 years before Christ. Today, people around the world struggle with unfulfilled expectations. They wrestle with the sense of emptiness, barrenness and loss when visions fail and hopes are crushed.

It is my desire to help people release the pain that occurs when those visions and hopes are dashed on the cruel rocks of reality. I want to inspire them to rise up and dream again, to birth their vision, embrace their journey and build their future.

I first preached this message on Hannah at my church, Freedom Chapel International Worship Center in Amityville, New York. I also shared it on the streets of New York City at our Rock the Block outreach and at The Brooklyn Tabernacle. While traveling internationally, I shared Hannah's miracle story at our crusades in the Dominican Republic, Tanzania and Kenya in East Africa.

Every time I preached "Miracles of a Misunderstood Woman," the response was overwhelming. People of all ages were captivated as they identified with Hannah's heart-breaking yet heroic story. Both men and women flooded the altars, responding with expectancy. Challenged to take hold of God's promise, they too thirsted for the miraculous power that Hannah received, to fulfill their own dreams and destiny.

As I locked myself into Hannah's story and stepped into the chapters of her life, I was mesmerized by her relentless passion to conceive a child against impossible odds. Although her story took place over 3,000 years ago, Hannah's desires and expectations are as relevant as the headlines of today's news.

Like many young girls, Hannah had hopes of marrying the perfect man, owning the perfect home and raising the perfect family. Unfortunately, her desires to live happily-ever-after were soon shattered when her dreams of motherhood were crushed.

The world tried to turn her reality into her identity. Though people saw her as barren, she refused to be identified by her condition, choosing instead to be identified by God's promise. Hannah had a life-changing choice to make. Would she allow her soul to be infected with bitterness, anguish and sorrow, or hold onto the hope that God would one day fulfill her heart's desire?

The distinctive dynamic of Hannah's miracle was that nothing stopped her. No opposition or obstacle could detour her. Every wall she faced, she either climbed over or broke through with the power of God. She overcame challenges through empowered vision and perseverance. Not only did her divine conception inspire me, but I believe it will inspire you!

God turned Hannah's bitterness into beauty, her misery into a miracle, her pain into praise, her sorrow into a song and her tragedy into triumph. Regardless of your gender or generation, if you have been marked, misunderstood, marred, or are in need of a miracle, this book is for you. It is my prayer that it would be a blessing to you.

Chapter 1
HANNAH'S MISSION

Oh LORD of hosts, if You will indeed look on the affliction of Your maidservant and remember me and not forget Your maidservant, but will give Your maidservant a male child, then I will give him to the LORD all the days of his life and no razor shall come upon his head (1 Samuel 1:11).

Hannah, wife of Elkanah, was a woman born with destiny in her heart. Her future was full of life, expectation and anticipation of what God had in store for her.

Our lives are like rivers teeming with divine encounters that flow into God's ocean of purpose and eternal plan. Her life, my life and your life are not a product of chance, but of divine design. In the Old Testament, God tells Jeremiah, "Before I formed you in the womb I knew you" (Jeremiah 1:5).

God has a calling for *each* of us. A calling that is unique and valuable intertwined with His strategic purpose on earth. The road He has ordained will have bumps, curves, mountains and valleys. Even through these trials, God is always at work developing us in preparation for each phase of our lives. He wants to teach us and cause us to experience the transformation and build a foundation needed to complete our unique mission.

Hannah had a sense of God's calling on her life, but had no idea of the cost. She was not aware that she would raise one of the greatest leaders in Israel's history. After 400 years of spiritual famine, Samuel would hear the voice of God and minister to a backslidden, wayward nation.

Hannah was born at a strategic time. She lived in the transition period between the deliverers of Israel, called "the judges," and the anointed kings that would follow her gifted son.

The Book of Judges was written in a time when Israel had no earthly king. Each time Israel fell into idolatry and disobedience, God would raise up a powerful leader to deliver them. Unfortunately, once the children of Israel were rescued, they never seemed to get the message to love only the Lord.

Samson was the final judge and deliverer in Israel. He judged during the high priest Eli's early years. The Book of Judges concludes 400 years of compromise and defiance with these words...

In those days there was no king in Israel; everyone did what was right in his own eyes (Judges 21:25).

Eli lacked the godly character to lead Israel or even discipline his sons. Israel's compromise began to permeate even the highest levels of power. Eli's sons, Hophni and Phineas, not only abused their power and defiled the offerings of the Lord (1 Samuel 2:12-14), but they walked in sexual immorality (1 Samuel 2:22). The Bible describes them this way...

Now the sons of Eli were corrupt; they did not know the Lord (1 Samuel 2:12).

It is against this backdrop that God sought a woman for His mission to birth a mighty leader. In His foreknowledge, God chose to pour His favor upon Hannah. In His prophetic design, God knew that she would faithfully play her part in His master plan of redemption. Despite much tribulation, she would accomplish this history-making task.

The name Hannah in Hebrew means favor: *Channâh, khan-naw'*, חַנָּה: *favored.*[1] God's favor doesn't come easily. It is birthed out of testing and remaining faithful to God through every trial you encounter. Your tested foundation of faith becomes a pathway of God's favor upon your life.

Hannah was a woman who was consistently tested by her barrenness, her adversaries, accusations and a self-centered husband. Still she remained faithful to the divine desire planted in her heart. In the process of time, God's favor would come upon her.

The plea in 1 Samuel 1:11 was Hannah's prayer to God, imploring His favor upon her life for a child. It arose from the heart of a young woman who wanted to be used by God. Her desire was not *just* to be a mother of a child to satisfy her own personal desire; her longing was much deeper than that. She had a vision for a son who would be used by God.

Her son, Samuel, would transition from Israel's last judge to the ministry of the priest. More than that, his most significant role would be that of a prophet who would call Israel back to faithfulness and anoint Israel's first two kings, Saul and David.

You Are a Miracle

Before the day we are conceived, God has a custom-made mission for each of us. The miracle of human conception is just that - a miracle. Think about how unique each one of us is. Each individual has his or her distinct retina scan, fingerprint and DNA.

How about the race to conception? On the day you were conceived, a single sperm out dueled, outmaneuvered and outran as many as 500 million others to cross the finish line to fertilize the egg. The fact that one out of 500 million completes the journey to form a new life demonstrates how miraculous you are. You are more than a *survivor*, you are a champion! Even though you were born into sin, sin did not stop God's amazing miracle of conception.

In God's eyes,

We are His workmanship, created in Christ Jesus, for good works which God prepared beforehand that we should walk in them (Ephesians 2:10).

However, over time many of us tune out of God's plan and tune in to the mainstream of American culture. The American dream frequency pounds out a relentless beat in modern society. We are taught to believe that esteem, career and financial success will bring us security, worth and happiness. Smothered and distorted by mountains of "stuff," we are often left feeling empty and unfulfilled.

In *Jesus Lives*, author Sarah Young writes, "The various means and measures of worldly 'success' pull on you constantly, leaving you in a fragmented, unfocused condition."[2] How true and relevant is this statement in our society today. It is only when we've been through the washing-machine cycles of life that many of us will stop and ponder the fundamental, universal questions of life, "Who am I?" and "Why am I here?"

People search for answers to these questions through various means: materialism, position, possession and even spiritual paths. The answer to these profound questions can only be found through a revelation from God and confirmed by His Word.

On November 4, 1984, through a life-threatening encounter, I surrendered my heart to Jesus Christ. I instantly had a revelation of "who I was" and "why I was here." I felt God's Spirit confirming that I was a child of God, created by God. Within 10 minutes of pondering that reality, the second question was answered. I knew I was here on this earth because God had a divine purpose for my life.

I had never read the Bible; but on that day, when I was given my first Bible, it came alive as I read it. God's Word became my love letter from heaven, which confirmed "who I was" and "why I was here."

I recently asked these questions to a retired, high-profile lawyer from Long Island. He brought his 25-year-old daughter, who was addicted to heroin, to get her into our Teen Challenge Ladies Program.

After sharing a message of hope and restoration with his precious daughter, I looked into the father's eyes and asked, "Who are you?" and "Why are you here?" His response was, "That's a pretty deep question."

Understand this. Here's a man who advised high-end businesses and the upper echelon of society. In every aspect he seemed very well off, but he did not have the answers to these simple yet real questions.

Thankfully, I had the opportunity to help him and his daughter realize who they are and how valuable they are to God.

This lawyer, like many people, had become distracted and lost sight of the fact that God had created him. He had not created himself.

Rick Warren, author of *The Purpose Driven Life*, shares,

> *The purpose of your life is far greater than your own personal fulfillment, your peace of mind or even your happiness. It's far greater than your family, your career, or even your wildest dreams and ambitions. If you want to know why you were placed on this planet, you must begin with God. You were born by His purpose and for His purpose.*[3]

The bottom line: The most important journey in life isn't finding yourself; it's discovering who God created you to be.

Think about how many people miss their God-ordained purpose because they are driven by the American dream. David Wong, a Chinese missionary to America said, "America is a monarchy. Her king is materialism, her queen is pleasure and her prince is entertainment." So many are driven to secure a career, rather than their mission from God. I often share with professionals, "Your career is not your mission. It's the vehicle you use to accomplish your mission. Never forget, *you* were supernaturally conceived in God's heart, formed by His hands and placed in this world for His purpose."

I don't believe Hannah really knew how significant her mission was, but

I'm certain she knew it was God's mission. She knew this was all that really mattered.

God Qualifies the Called

Throughout biblical history, God selected the most unlikely candidates for the most incredible miracles. There was Sarah and Abraham, to whom God promised a child, despite their old age. When Abraham was 100 years old and Sarah 90, God fulfilled His promise and blessed them with a miracle baby named Isaac.

There was also Rahab, a harlot whom God chose to help defeat Jericho city and pave the way for the Children of Israel to reach the Promised Land. She was divinely engrafted into God's family and through her lineage, eight generations later, Jesus Christ was born.

There was Mary Magdalene, a woman from whom Jesus cast out seven demons. After this, she might not be considered a reliable witness, but God chose her to be the first to proclaim Jesus' resurrection.

Beloved, we see that God does not call the qualified; He qualifies the called. If He did it for them, He will do it for you, regardless of your past or present circumstances.

God's Assignment

When God reveals your calling, a fire is ignited within you. That fire is maintained by the fuel of your passion for your mission. A person with a passion is completely dedicated to a cause and cannot rest until the mission is accomplished. Although many people around you may think your cause is unattainable, your passion will remind others that,

With God all things are possible (Matthew 19:26).

Hannah's life was driven by her passion to bear a son that would honor her husband and be used by God.

Agnes Gonxha Bojaxhiu is an example of a young woman whom God ignited with a cause. Her passion set her on a mission, even though many thought she was foolish.

"Agnes felt called to ministry when she was a teenager. She did her ministerial training in Ireland and India. One day she approached her superiors with a God-ordained passion. She said, 'I have three pennies and a dream from God to build an orphanage.'

Her superiors said, 'You can't build an orphanage with three pennies. With

three pennies you can't do anything.'

Agnes smiled and said, 'I know. But with God and three pennies I can do anything.' For fifty years Agnes worked among the poor in the slums of Calcutta, India. In 1979, the woman we know as Mother Teresa won the Nobel Peace Prize.

Toward the end of her ministry, Mother Teresa was often asked by admirers how they could make a difference with their own lives the way she had with hers. Mother Teresa's oft-repeated response was four words long: 'Find your own Calcutta.'"[4]

Remember, if you shoot for nothing, you'll hit it every time. If you shoot for the heavens, you're bound to hit a star.

As we follow Hannah's dramatic journey to her miracle, we see that she faced many trials, but remained true to her mission. Everything she experienced built her character and prepared her to become a *woman of miracles*. This journey is not just one mother's take on a difficult path. It is God's road map to guide *our* passage and prepare *us* for the mighty vision He has entrusted to each one of us.

People God Uses

Throughout the pages of Scripture, we see how God used people who were inadequate to teach a lesson or accomplish an impossible goal. Consider some of the people from the Bible that God chose to fulfill His purposes.

After the Flood, Noah planted a vineyard, made wine, got drunk and cursed one of his sons.

> Abraham lied under pressure.
> Jacob was a hustler.
> Jepthah was rejected.
> Leah was ugly.
> Rachel was a liar.
> Joseph was abused.
> Moses stuttered.
> Gideon was insecure.
> Samson was lustful.
> Rahab was a prostitute.
> David was an adulterer.
> Elijah was suicidal.
> Jeremiah was depressed.

Nehemiah was criticized.
Jonah was afraid.
Naomi was a widow.
Hosea's wife was unfaithful.
Job was traumatized.
Peter was hard-headed.
Martha was a worrier.
Thomas was doubtful.
Paul persecuted the church.
Timothy was fearful.
Mark was annoying.
Philip was double-minded.
James and John were angry.

And the Samaritan woman had five ex-husbands.

Thankfully, God *still* uses the foolish things of the world to confound the wise. He has a habit of picking nobodies and making them somebodies, as the apostle Paul proclaimed…

For you see your calling, brethren, that not many wise according to the flesh, not many mighty, not many noble, are called. But God has chosen the foolish things of the world to put to shame the wise and God has chosen the weak things of the world to put to shame the things which are mighty; (1 Corinthians 1:26, 27).

What concerns have you brought to God lately? When was the last time you felt spiritually and emotionally drained or discouraged and said, "I just can't do it!"? Let me remind you that if you feel inadequate or that something seems impossible, you are not alone.

I recently read, "If your path seems lowly and difficult, it's because of your high calling." In studying and personally knowing great men and women who accomplished great feats, I have realized that the greater the calling, the greater the trials. Nothing great in life comes easy.

Mama Jack Called

Like Hannah, my mother's life and experience were guided by the mission she had in her heart. Growing up in the era of the Civil Rights Movement, my mother couldn't bear to stand by and watch as African-American families were abused, mocked and treated like trash. Known to her many "adopted" multicultural families as Mama Jack, she was driven by a passion to fight against social injustice and to see all people receive equal rights and opportunities.

In the 1960s, my mother and father, along with their nine children (apparently barrenness wasn't an issue for them) moved to an area of Long Island, New York that bordered the black community. We weren't bothered by it because we were "color" blind.

A block from our house was a grocery store where my mother enjoyed shopping. While shopping for all eleven of us, she began to bond with the African-American women who also shopped and worked there. She spent quality time on the "other side of the fence" and developed many friendships. When mom saw the oppression that they faced, she became burdened with their plight.

Her *burden* transformed into a *mission* to seek change. She got involved with the Civil Rights Movement and helped establish the Civil Rights Council in our town. Their team invited Dr. Martin Luther King, Jr. to speak in three of our towns in Long Island. In fact, the leadership council meetings for these events were held at my home. The final meeting, in which Dr. Martin Luther King, Jr. attended, was scheduled to be in my home, but it grew so large they had to move it to the high school.

Discrimination in the school system provoked my mother to also join other concerned citizens in the community to start local chapters of the NAACP (National Association for the Advancement of Colored People) and CORE (Congress of Racial Equality). These groups called for open enrollment and racial balance in schools.

They fought against the State Housing Authority's proposal to build projects in the black community that would segregate them from their white neighbors. The town even went as far as building a 10-foot fence between the two communities to hide the black people. My mother and her fellow members took the fight all the way to the state capital, Albany, New York. Their efforts resulted in the elimination of the fence and a revised building plan that met the needs of the black community.

My mother also participated in the NAACP, CORE and The Poor People's Campaign plan to take a large group of people to the famous march in Washington, D.C. There, they joined Dr. Martin Luther King, Jr. at the Lincoln Memorial on August 28, 1963, as he preached his historic "I Have a Dream" message. The first Long Island organizational meeting for the march took place in our dining room. My mother and the Rockville Centre contingents made hundreds of bologna sandwiches to feed those who traveled to Washington with a mission of hope, healing and freedom.

This was the beginning of my mother's heroic journey, which led her down a painful road. It changed not only her life, but our entire family as well.

Mission Possible

One of the unintended casualties of my mother's activism was the rejection that my family faced. Unable to process that rejection, I turned to drugs to numb the pain, but God rescued me from that life of destruction and addiction. In 1985, I graduated from Brooklyn Teen Challenge, a Christ-centered drug and alcohol program founded by David Wilkerson, author of *The Cross and Switchblade*. Since its inception in 1958, Teen Challenge has grown into the largest, most successful program in the world with over 1,400 programs in over 120 countries.

I am so thankful to God for restoring my life and giving *me* a vision to reach the lost. That *vision* became *my mission,* to bring God's love and hope to broken young people and families around the world. My mother's mission was passed on to me.

Like Hannah, who experienced much brokenness in her life, I have learned that miracles are often birthed at the brink of brokenness. God humbles us at certain times to align us. Have you been there? I've been there.

I remember a few years ago when God called me to build a new church. It was one of the greatest challenges of my life, especially when funding went dry and it seemed like all of my key people were quitting on me. I was at my wit's end. I often went into the woods for my prayer time, weeping and crying out to God. It wasn't the first time I hit ground zero.

Many times over the last 25 years I have struggled through moments of futility and weakness. All my skill sets were depleted and I was empty. Every time I came to the end of my strength, I cried out in my brokenness, "I can't."

It was at times like these when the Holy Spirit whispered in my heart, "*Now* you can because '*My strength* is made perfect in [your] weakness'" (2 Corinthians 12:9). "Now rise. I am with you!" I have learned, when you reach the end of your rope, tie a knot and hold on because things are sometimes at their worst just before the breakthrough.

These encounters fueled my faith with fresh passion to boldly pursue God's promise. Only then was I able to rise up with supernatural power as God accomplished the impossible.

Futility does not have to be the end. It can be fertile ground for God to do a new thing. Desperation can remind you of who you are in God and who God is in you. "You may never know that Jesus is all you need, until Jesus is all you have."

When it became apparent to Hannah that she was barren, her request to God seemed impossible. Yet, she still sought God for a child; and, in her plea, the purity of her heart was revealed. The inner longing was not just to have a son for herself or her husband. Her prayer revealed that deep in her soul she knew God had a plan for her life. She would have a son not for *man*, but for *God's* purpose.

Have you experienced this cry in your life? Have you come before God with a mission in your heart, a burden that you truly believe is from Him? When all your circumstances make it seem impossible, when all your resources are depleted and your support system is gone, remember that *God has not abandoned you.*

If your mission is from God, but the journey seems unbearable, do not despair. When you are down to nothing, God is up to something. This is where your walk of faith is tested. Many of you have heard or used the phrase, "We walk by faith, not by sight" (2 Corinthians 5:7). This is not a cliché; it's a command from God's Word.

Corrie ten Boom stated, "Faith in God sees the invisible, believes the incredible and receives the impossible."[5] Know this, "Faith does not operate in the realm of possible. There is no glory for God in that which is humanly possible. Faith begins where man's power ends."[6]

The Dash Between the Dates

I have been privileged and somewhat burdened to officiate at funerals for over 25 years. Every time I looked at a tombstone, two things stood out. First, I quickly calculated the person's age. Second, I thought about the dash in between the dates and how this person may have lived his/her life. If there was a scanner to read the dash, what would it reveal?

On a tombstone you will see the date of birth and the date of death. The only mystery is the dash. Triumph and tragedy occur in the dash between the dates. Destiny is discovered, detoured or discarded there. The tragedy is that all too often the dash represents the unwritten poems, uncompleted songs and half-realized dreams.

For some, it only offered the disappointment of *should have done, could have done* and *would have done*. But for Hannah, there were no such excuses. Hannah's mission is a reminder to all that God always hears us when we call, especially during our times of affliction.

Her life story, as we will see, is an example of a woman struck with failure, who found that her failure was not final. Full of faith and fortitude, Hannah's dash defines a woman who fought the good fight and faithfully fulfilled her dream.

It was Hannah's destiny to give birth to Samuel, but his birth was not what defined her. A person's destiny does not define his/her life. It is the *journey* that *leads* him/her to their destiny that shapes his/her character and defines his/her life.

Hannah had a hunger for God and a heart's desire for a son. She believed, even in her barrenness, that God would make it happen. We live in a world that dreams of "happily ever after's." In God's kingdom, we do have a promise of a joy-filled eternity, but we also face problems along the way. Even though Hannah's journey would not be a sunshine-paved road of ease to a miracle, her faithfulness to the mission would result in the birth of Samuel.

As we consider the tremendous results of Hannah's faith, let us examine the rough, rocky roads and map the minefield that would lead her to the miracle. Follow me as we examine the life of this misunderstood woman and her quest for her miracle son.

CHAPTER 2

A MARRIED WOMAN

Now there was a certain man of Ramathaim Zophim, of the mountains of Ephraim and his name was Elkanah…And he had two wives: the name of one was Hannah (1 Samuel 1:1, 2).

Almost every little girl dreams of the day when her perfect man will come to sweep her off her feet in his strong, yet gentle loving arms. Together they glide across the clouds of passion into the romantic sunset. She envisions the moment when her life will change forever. She walks down the aisle toward her beloved in an elegant white wedding dress. With her train flowing behind her, they embrace their covenant in the sunrise of their destiny.

Hannah had many of the timeless dreams that young girls have today. When she reached the age of betrothal, she dreamed of the life that she and her husband would create together. This fantasy is not just a little girl's dream, but a mother's and father's dream as well. A mother's vision is to see her precious little girl grow toward womanhood and find the perfect mate.

Similarly, as a father tenderly holds his baby girl's hands, lifting her up, he places her tiny feet on top of his. As they dance together, he pictures that special day when he will release her into the hands of her loving husband to start a family of their own. This timeless dream was shared by every Hebrew girl for thousands of years, even as it is today.

As a father, since both my daughters were babies, I have always prayed that they find the husband that God has for them. My daughter, Dominique, at 18 years old and a freshman in college, shared her heart's description of the "perfect man" in this letter to Jesus:

Dear Lord,

I come before You today asking if You would please hear my prayer. Since I was a little girl, I've prayed about the man that You would bring alongside me. I just can't help but wonder how I will truly know who he is when he steps into my life. I know he is going to be amazing, and I pray that the desires You have placed in my heart for the kind of man I need will help me discern who he is.

The first quality I plan to look for is his character. Do others see him as a man of God? Loving, gentle, kind, caring, compassionate and generous. I don't want to base my decisions on other's opinions, but I imagine people being able to see God in him without him even trying to let it show.

I pray that he will accept me for who I am and love everything about me, flaws and all. Not only will he love me, but I pray that he will love You, Lord. That he would learn how to respect and treat me the way You would, so it feels as if You are pursuing me.

I pray that our futures will intertwine in our mission to serve You. That my dreams will relate to his, so that our two worlds will collide for Your glory and we can serve the Lord together with both of our hearts.

I see him with many other qualities as well: a positive mindset, a fun attitude and an outgoing way about himself. I see him being strong, independent, handsome and "Mr. Fix It," ready to fix my car or our house when needed. I see myself being able to turn to him for advice and help. I have this feeling that I am going to be able to respect him so much.

I desire my husband to have a heart for the lost, always wanting to help and restore hope to someone who needs it. This means he will not only be wise, but a good listener, able to hear the heart of the hurting.

Most of all, Lord, I just pray that this person, whoever he is, will be my best friend, someone I can laugh with and share crazy moments with. Someone who is daring and adventurous. Someone I can feel completely comfortable around and who helps me feel secure about who I am.

I pray that we will have this amazing connection where he will know my thoughts and I will know what he is about to say, a "finishing-my-sentences" kind of love. And, of course, I know he'll be a great father to our children.

I do have some fears from the past in regard to true love, which have caused me to put up a wall around my heart. I pray that when my future husband comes into my life, that he will be able to break those guards down. I understand that this will only happen in Your timing. Restore the trust that I almost lost hope in.

I am willing to wait for my other half for however long it takes. I trust in You, Lord, to guide me when he comes my way, teaching me not only how to love him the way he deserves and desires, but to look at his heart and not just his outer appearance. Guide us both on the road to love in Your timing. Let him have a strong conviction of Your truth.

Hear my prayer, Lord,

Dominique

Between each line of Dominique's prayer, you can feel her heart beat with passionate expectations. As we take a look into the Hebrew marriage tradition and the ceremony, you'll sense the same holy excitement that Hannah experienced as a young Hebrew bride.

The Big Day

For a young girl in Israel, the first step toward marriage was betrothal. Hannah was delighted to find out that Elkanah, son of Jeroham, was going to be her fiancé. He was a fine, young Ephraimite. The very thought of his name thrilled her because in Hebrew *Elkanah*, 'Elqanah,' "(הָנְקְלאֶ) means God has purchased."[1]

On the day that her prospective bridegroom was coming to propose, Hannah was giddy with excitement as Elkanah travelled from his father's house in Mount Ephraim to her home in Ramah, just five miles north of Jerusalem. As he met with her father, she strained her ears to hear their negotiations on the price he would pay to purchase his bride, known in Hebrew as the *mohar*. From the moment he paid the dowry, their marriage covenant was established. They were regarded as husband and wife.

These were days of excitement and anticipation. Hannah was now declared to be consecrated and set apart exclusively for her bridegroom. According to Hebrew tradition, they drank from a cup of wine over which their betrothal benediction had been pronounced. As she looked into her groom's handsome eyes, sparkling in the candlelight, she longed for their "happily ever after." Then, as quickly as the moment came, it passed, for Elkanah was required to return to his father's house.

Her heart pounded and yet she felt emptiness in the pit of her stomach. She watched him mount his camel and leave for the land of the Ephraimites. There, Elkanah remained separated from his wife for twelve months, as required by Hebrew law to establish a marriage covenant. Under the Law, this separation represented a time of *purification,* but for Hannah, it was a time of anticipation.

The Law prescribed a year of betrothal to prove that the bride was not pregnant. For Hannah, it was her opportunity to demonstrate her purity, love and faithfulness to her beloved. As his silhouette faded on the horizon, she found herself longing for his return.

During that year Hannah prepared for married life, busying herself as she gathered all the essentials for her future home. At the same time Elkanah was occupied, preparing their accommodations in his father's house. There he would bring his bride to live with him after their period of separation.

The next step for Hannah was the ceremonial cleansing, called the *Mikveh*. She was taught that the *Mikveh* was not about *uncleanness*, but a ritual that brought human beings into contact with the power of the Holy God. All the rules of marriage were governed by the Talmud דוּמְלַת, the record of rabbinic discussions pertaining to Jewish law, ethics, philosophy, customs and history. They provided the central text of traditional Jewish faith.

According to the Talmud, the ultimate source of water was the river that emerged from Eden. By participating in the *Mikveh*, women symbolically believed that they were immersing themselves in the wholeness of Eden and were emerging reborn and pure like Adam and Eve. *Mikveh* also represented the physical source of life. As Hannah emerged from the waters of *Mikveh*, she had a keen expectation that her womb would one day produce Elkanah's first son and the fruit of their love.[2]

At the end of the year, it was the custom for the groom, best man and other male escorts to leave the grooms father's house and conduct a torchlight procession to the bride's home. The formal process of consummating the marriage came to a crescendo with the *taking of the bride* referred to as the *nissuin* (literally "taking").

Hannah knew about the traditional *abduction* and that it would occur in the middle of the night. Elkanah and his cohorts set out in the night, making every attempt to completely surprise her and her maidens.

This was the romantic anticipation that many Jewish brides looked forward to, being "stolen" by their husbands-to-be. On many occasions, Hannah and her girlfriends discussed her "abduction," giggling in glee at the thrill of being carried off into the night by the one whom she loved. Although she was expecting her groom to come for her, she did not know the exact time.

Her anticipation mounted when she heard that on the Shabbat (Sabbath Service) of that week, Elkanah had prayed in synagogue. Each week, a different portion of the Torah and the Prophets was read in synagogue. It was customary for the groom to have the honor of reciting a blessing over the Torah, called the *aliyah*, one week before his wedding. Hannah trembled as she laid out her veil and dress, waiting, making sure that she was prepared for the coming of her groom.

The groom and his attendants grabbed torches to light the way through the dark streets of the town to the house of the bride. The abduction was considered romantic, completely surprising the bride as they burst into the house in the middle of the night. Her heart pounded with excitement when she heard the blowing of the *shofar*, a traditional trumpet made from a ram's horn. Suddenly as they crossed the threshold, the groom's party announced their arrival with a shout, "Behold, the bridegroom cometh!"

Hannah's face flushed with expectancy as Elkanah swept her into his arms. Together with her female attendants, the enlarged wedding party returned in a celebratory procession, from her father's house to the home of Elkanah's father. The night was magical. Elaborately clothed, they were treated like a king and queen, even being adorned with crowns.

Upon their arrival, the wedding party found the guests already assembled in celebration. She breathlessly followed the ceremony as she waited for the moment when they would be escorted by the wedding party to the bridal chamber. Prior to entering the chamber, she remained veiled so that no one could see her face.

They would be married under a canopy called the *huppah*. The *huppah* served as a booth, separating the wedding circle from the hustle of the street while creating a sacred space.

In Talmudic tradition, it was customary to plant a cedar tree representing majesty, strength and height at the birth of a boy and a cypress tree representing beauty and grace at the birth of a girl. Both trees also represented longevity and life. The *huppah* poles, which held up the corners of their canopy, were made from branches cut from the trees. Elkanah took Hannah inside to symbolize her coming under his authority and protection and to have privacy for the consummation of their marriage.

While the groomsmen and bridesmaids waited outside, Elkanah and Hannah entered the bridal chamber alone. There, in the privacy of that place, they for the first time entered into physical union, thereby consummating the marriage covenant that was made 12 months before.

Afterward, Elkanah made the announcement through the curtain to his friends in the wedding party that the marriage had been consummated. The word quickly spread throughout the crowd. Hannah could hear her closest friends passing on the news of their marital union to the other wedding guests.

As the shouts rang in the city, Hannah could hear the sound of music and gaiety as the wedding guests received the good news. She softly lay back on her pillow, closed her eyes and sighed in happy exhilaration that her dream had come true. For the next seven days they would feast around the city, fellowship and celebrate Jehovah's blessing on their marriage. Hannah's delight wandered back and forth between the excitement of her marital union and the anticipation of what was to come. Now, with the veil removed, everyone could see her delight at the blessing of her marriage.

Hannah went to live in her father-in-law's home with her new husband. She could barely contain herself, waiting for the day when they would leave his home and set up housekeeping on their own. She remembered the seven blessings that they prayed during the ceremony. Each blessing began with, *Blessed be the Lord our God, King of the Universe who…*

- *Created everything for His glory.*
- *Fashioned the Man.*
- *Fashioned the Man in His image and prepared for Him, from Himself, a building for eternity.*
- *May the barren one exalt and jubilantly rejoice through the regathering of her children amidst her in gladness. Blessed art thou who makes Zion rejoice with her children.*
- *Gladdens groom and bride.*
- *Created joy and gladness, groom and bride, rejoicing, glad song, pleasure, delight, love, brotherhood, peace and companionship.*
- *Creator of the fruit of the vine.*[3]

Today, the marriage tradition is often changed, challenged and compromised. I've seen couples get married while skydiving and bungee jumping, even some of the craziest venues and stunts that you can imagine. The marriage covenant has been exploited through television shows, like *Bridezilla* that depicts controlling, selfish, disrespectful brides who demean their groom, bridesmaids and family to get their way.

The world may find this humorous, but God has a standard for His holy marriage covenant. It represents the union of Jesus as the Groom and His church as the Bride.

I've had the privilege of officiating at some of the most beautiful, holy weddings where the sanctuary reflects heaven's throne room and the bride and groom reflect the fullness of Christ and His church.

I'm not opposed to the nontraditional venues. I've had the opportunity to marry couples on a lakeside or in banquet halls. I understand a couple's enthusiasm and passion to do it differently; however, it's not the venue that God's concerned about. It's the covenant vows that mean everything.

Like many marriages, when the honeymoon is over, imperfections begin to surface. When God established marriage, His covenant principle was "these two shall become one."

> *And Adam said: 'This is now bone of my bone and flesh of my flesh; she shall be called woman, Because she was taken out of Man.' Therefore, a man shall leave his father and mother and be joined to his wife and they shall become one flesh* (Genesis 2:23, 24).

I remember the teaching from Genesis that my wife, Miriam, and I received prior to our marriage. "A man shall leave, cleave and become one." I have heard it in many marriage encounters and in counseling over the years and it still applies today.

Marriage is not just a commitment, but a covenant with God that comes with many challenges. When I do pre-marriage and post-marriage counseling, I remind the couple that the two most important covenants in a person's life are the covenant of salvation and the covenant of marriage.

I often refer to a salvation verse and paraphrase it to the marriage covenant. The Bible says, "Work out your salvation with fear and trembling" (Philippians 2:12). If that is true of our salvation, we must also work out our marriage with fear and trembling.

Marriage and family expectations, as defined in Dominique's prayer letter, are not always what one prayed for or dreamed about. With the responsibilities of life, living in a stress-filled environment with physical challenges, conflicts arise and expectations can be deflated.

In marriage these obstacles are a reality that a covenant commitment with God and each other can overcome. Hannah was about to face this overwhelming reality.

Dream Come True

When Elkanah carried her over the threshold of their first home, Hannah's eyes gleamed with delight. What a beautiful home and wonderful husband. What an exciting life. Tears of joy filled her eyes as he took a plain gold ring and placed it on her finger, reciting *"Behold you are sanctified (betrothed) to me with this ring, according to the Law of Moses and Israel."*[4]

She smiled, looking lovingly at the ring, knowing that it symbolized the groom encompassing, protecting and providing for her. Her life was happy and her future was secure. She was living the dream. As nervousness crept in, she promised herself, "I will satisfy my husband. I will be a wonderful mother and devoted wife."

Hannah was determined to keep that promise. As a new wife, she delighted in every visit to the market. She skipped through the marketplace with joy and expectation. The fragrance of baked goods, fresh fish and fruits filled the air. She moved through the hustle and bustle of the frantic shoppers, oblivious to the crushing crowd and noisy streets. Her countenance glowed with love and her rosy cheeks were gleaming.

Carrying her woven basket, she carefully chose the best fruits, vegetables, meats and bread. She sensed every woman's eyes on her, certain that they wished they could have the joy that she had with Elkanah. All that remained was for her to bear him a son.

The dream that Hannah held onto from a young age began with such promise, but she was headed toward hardship. She was about to face her worst nightmare, the prospect that she might never have a child and be unable to fulfill the fourth blessing "exalt and jubilantly rejoice through the regathering of her children."[5]

She would be forced to endure the ridicule of others, the stigma of society and the pain of her own lost dreams. It would be in this place that Hannah would either collapse under the weight of disappointment, or cry out to God and hold on to the vision of motherhood.

CHAPTER 3

A MARKED WOMAN

But to Hannah he would give a double portion, for he loved Hannah, although the LORD had closed her womb (1 Samuel 1:5).

This picture-perfect marriage, vibrant and filled with excitement, was about to face tremendous trials. Each day Hannah strived to be the perfect wife as she supervised the household and cared for her husband. But at the end of each month, as the "time of women" passed, she began to grow nervous about still not carrying her beloved's child.

Although the journey of their early marriage years is not detailed in the Bible, Hannah's story unfolds between the lines of Scripture. The author, Samuel, inspired by God, reflects on some of the scenes of his mother's marriage in 1 Samuel 1.

Hannah's dream of motherhood began to fade as she faced the harsh reality of being childless. As months turned into years, the women of the town began to watch her more closely. The village gossips put their heads together asking, "Where is the son Hannah's supposed to bear for Elkanah?" Some began to conclude that her womb was closed and that she would never bear a child for her husband. At best, she was physically inferior, or at worst, Jehovah God was displeased with her and thus punishing her for some unknown sin.

It hurt her deeply when some suggested that her husband was not man enough to father a child. She secretly began to struggle with a deepening sense of inadequacy as she wondered, "What's wrong with me?" The fear of being barren now haunted Hannah. At a time when infertility earned a woman both scorn and ridicule, this was becoming her reality.

Hannah was now a marked woman. The town busybodies singled her out, branding her a childless wife. She was segregated and considered an outsider. She no longer felt like one of them.

This shift from envied woman to misfit underscores the beginning of a terrible stigma. Hannah was looked upon as an inferior female to mothers and wives. She was regarded as a half-a-woman therefore half-a-wife.

Insecurity and Self-doubt

At some point in life, most people will feel the pain of being an outsider. All of us have an inherent need to belong to something. When we are ostracized, the feelings of insecurity and self-doubt take over. Peer pressure can have more of an impact on us than we could ever imagine.

- Why does 1 out of every 3 teenage girls in America have an eating disorder?
- Why do young girls cut themselves, taking their anger and pain out on their own flesh?
- Why do so many college students binge drink?
- Why are teens getting hooked on pain medication?
- Why is suicide the third leading cause of death among teens?
- Why are people obsessed with plastic surgery?
- Why do millions of Americans spend billions of dollars on vanity products they don't need?[1]

Why? Because they are willing to spend money they don't have, participate in risky behavior and harm themselves, just to fit in and avoid social disgrace. In the end, some even choose death at their own hands, rather than endure the continuous pain of life. Today, some women endure multiple plastic surgeries in an effort to feel like they measure up. In Hannah's day, the response to social pressure may have been different, but the pain of rejection and bullying remains the same. The condition of fallen humanity has not and will not change.

The Role of Women

To truly understand the depth of the hurt and shame that Hannah endured, we must try to understand how the Hebrew culture viewed barrenness. She faced the onslaught of two overwhelming forces that seemed to conspire against her: the Hebrew culture and the Jewish faith.

Today in the United States, we celebrate the creativity and potential of women. However in Old Testament Israel, women were considered inferior. They held the lowest position, were not permitted to testify in court and were viewed as barely above a slave. Married women were completely subservient to their husbands, to the point of being considered his property.

Although women had many functions within the home, society saw their main purpose as conceiving children and raising a family. A couple's aspiration was to give birth to a healthy *male* child. The oldest male would inherit the greatest portion of his father's estate, as well as rulership over his home. The social status of a woman was raised considerably when she gave birth. Mothers were given increased privilege and respect. The more children a wife had, the greater her status.

Since Hannah was barren, she remained on the bottom rung of the social ladder, marked by failure and disappointment. Legally, a barren woman could not even secure the proper distribution of her husband's wealth.

Motherhood was also synonymous with femininity. If a woman was unable to have children, she was seen as being deprived of the very thing that made her female. All of these stigmas led to great dishonor and insecurity for a barren woman.

Rejection and Shame

Like Hannah, my mother and our family experienced the stigma of being outcasts because of our involvement in the Civil Rights Movement. At a time in America when racial tensions were high, my mother allowed a black family, the Angelstons, who had lost their home to a fire, to come live with us. This decision made our views on racial equality even more obvious. We were one of the few white families accepted by the black community.

When the Angelstons eventually moved out, we emotionally adopted another black family into our home – the Smiths. When Mrs. Smith passed away, we became one big family. Since they lived only four blocks away, our house became their house and their house became our house. *Mi casa es su casa* was not just a cliché or term of endearment; it was the real thing.

Another special young black brother named Bobby Lloyd was also grafted into our family. Bobby was like an older brother to me. He was a street fighter, gangster and major heroin/cocaine dealer in Harlem and Long Island. At the same time, he was our guardian angel. At 18 years old, Bobby escorted my mother and father to the march in Washington, D.C. to hear Dr. Martin Luther King, Jr.'s speech. Whenever there was trouble in the house, Bobby was there to protect us. My father nicknamed him, "The Black Knight."

While we developed close relationships with our black brothers and sisters, most of the white families in the neighborhood rejected us. We endured constant verbal abuse. We were marked, ridiculed and insulted. We heard it and felt it every day.

I remember at the age of six, when my friends on the block went to their friends' backyard, I would have to stop at the front gate and not go further. I knew I wasn't allowed on my white neighbors' property.

When there were birthday parties, I was never invited. I would stand across the street, watching my friends laugh and splash in their pools, having fun. I wasn't allowed to go swimming with them because they thought I would pollute the water. Even though there were times my friends snuck me into their houses when their parents weren't home, I always felt scared, uncomfortable and out of place.

Our neighbors branded us dirty people and low-lifes. Even the police department mocked us. When they arrested my friends, they would say, "Don't hang out with the Jack family. They're bad people."

In high school, graffiti on the bathroom walls declared, "The Jacks are n*gg*r lovers." As I heard the whispering and mocking behind my back, it increased my feelings of inferiority. The only way to hide them was to sedate myself. In fact, all of my family began to numb their pain with drugs, alcohol and co-dependent relationships. Yet in spite all of the pain, we continued to hold onto our relationships with the African-American people that we loved so dearly.

The Sting of Rejection

Some of you know what it's like to feel rejected, alone and ridiculed because of what you believe in. Are there days you struggle just to hang on to your vision?

When you take a stand, firm in your faith, you can expect to undergo persecution for what you believe. When society tells you that your dreams are impossible and yet you continue to fight for them, you can expect to experience repercussions. My mother was forced to endure it and so was Hannah.

The apostle Peter solemnly declares,

Beloved, do not think it strange concerning the fiery trial which is to try you, as though some strange thing happened to you (1 Peter 4:12).

Even Jesus endured persecution. He told His disciples…

If you were of the world, the world would love its own. Yet because you are not of the world, but I chose you out of the world, therefore the world hates you. Remember the word that I said to you, 'A servant is not greater than his master.' If they persecuted Me, they will also persecute you (John 15:19, 20).

Along with having to deal with the social stigma of being childless, Hannah had to cope with the religious labels placed on her by her culture. In the Old Testament, under the Law, barrenness was seen as a punishment or curse from God.

Can you hear the local leaders and the town busybodies reminding her of the promises that weren't being fulfilled like in Exodus...

So you shall serve the LORD *your God and He will bless your bread and your water. And I will take sickness away from the midst of you. No one shall suffer miscarriage or be barren in your land; I will fulfill the number of your days*
(Exodus 23:25, 26).

Similarly, Deuteronomy promised that if Israel followed God's commands, they would...

Be blessed above all peoples; there shall not be a male or female barren among you or among your livestock (Deuteronomy 7:14).

These Scriptures reinforced and justified the community's interpretation of Hannah's barrenness as a judgment from God. Hannah was marked a "sinner" and viewed by some as an enemy of the Almighty.

It is obvious that Hannah was dealing with more than just being without a child. She was enduring social stigma and religious judgments, as well as the pain of an unfulfilled dream. She constantly endured the accusation that she would *never* be a *virtuous* woman for her husband and the rest of her family, friends and neighbors.

The word *virtuous*, chayil לַיִח – in Hebrew means valor, wealth, strength, force, power, or efficient. It was used to describe a righteous Hebrew woman who was not just a faithful wife, but even more, a faithful *mother.*[2]

Solomon used the phrase "virtuous woman" while penning the 31st chapter of the Book of Proverbs, long after Hannah's time. In Solomon's masterpiece on womanhood, he described the role of a virtuous wife and mother. Attaining these attributes was the goal and calling of every Hebrew woman.

I'm sure Hannah personified Solomon's definition of a virtuous wife in Proverbs 31:10-14:

Who can find a virtuous wife?

For her worth is far above rubies.

The heart of her husband safely trusts her;

So he will have no lack of gain.
She does him good and not evil
All the days of her life.
She seeks wool and flax,
And willingly works with her hands.
She is like the merchant ships,
She brings her food from afar.

Solomon then goes on to define the role of motherhood, a woman caring for her children, as a "household" in verses 15–28. Although this Scripture was written 100 years after Hannah's time, these characteristics were the standards of her day.

At this point, it seemed that Hannah might never fulfill this role. She was forced to deal with the emotional impact of her inability to live up to the expectations of a culture that viewed these characteristics as the epitome of womanhood. Without bearing children, she could never be the "virtuous mother" described by Solomon:

She also rises while it is yet night,
And provides food for her household,
And a portion for her maidservants.
She considers a field and buys it;
From her profits she plants a vineyard.
She girds herself with strength,
And strengthens her arms…
She is not afraid of snow for her household,
For all her household is clothed with scarlet.
She makes tapestry for herself;
Her clothing is fine linen and purple.
Her husband is known in the gates,
When he sits among the elders of the land…
She watches over the ways of her household,
And does not eat the bread of idleness.

Her children rise up and call her blessed;

Her husband also and he praises her.

The verse, "Her husband is known in the gates, when he sits among the elders of the land" illustrates another great social difficulty Hannah had to face.

How did society view Elkanah and how did this situation affect him? Was he also marked? What did the elders at the gates think? Undoubtedly, Hannah served him with excellence, honor and loving care. To those at the gates, did they think he was a fool to love a barren woman? Painfully, she was forced to watch her husband go through the ridicule of having a wife that was unable to conceive as well as the accusations that he couldn't produce an heir.

Although Hannah may not have been schooled in the Torah, she was familiar with the stories of barren women in Genesis, such as Sarah, Rebekah and Rachel, the wives of Abraham, Isaac and Jacob, whom God miraculously made fertile again. She persisted in her belief that God would one day give her a child *if* He so desired. She consoled herself with the thought that it was *His choice* not to allow her to have children *at this time in her life*.

Even though Elkanah may have misunderstood Hannah, nowhere does it indicate that he mistreated her. Scripture specifically indicates that Elkanah "loved Hannah, although the LORD had closed her womb" (1 Samuel 1:5). He demonstrated his love for her by offering a double portion sacrifice to the Lord on Hannah's behalf.

Still, he had to deal with the insecurity that came from not having an heir to carry on his name or inherit his wealth. It was common in the Old Testament to have more than one wife. Despite this, I believe Elkanah would have remained married exclusively to Hannah had she been able to produce an heir to carry on his lineage.

I Need a Baby Mama

The Scriptures are not clear as to how many years Hannah tried to conceive before another woman eventually came into the picture. Was it after the second or third year, the fourth or fifth year? Unfortunately, the Bible does not provide a conclusive timeline showing how long he waited, but the Scriptures clearly illustrate Elkanah's demonstration of love toward his wife. We can confidently conclude that he patiently waited for her to conceive.

Nevertheless, the heartbreaking decision was looming on the horizon. Traditional Hebrew pressure would have forced Elkanah to find another woman to preserve his lineage and fulfill his calling to fatherhood. Hannah knew the decision was imminent, but tried to hold on to her hope, believing that God would bless her with a child.

Hannah consoled herself with the fact that releasing Elkanah to have another wife, in order to procreate, was just a cultural tradition. "This is something I will have to endure *momentarily,*" she thought. Surely, the time would come when she would bear the promised heir and all would regret their criticism during this difficult time.

It finally became obvious that welcoming a second wife into the home was inevitable. Doubt may have begun to creep into Hannah's heart. The dynamic of her marriage was about to change. Elkanah was no longer going to be exclusively hers and their intimacy would suffer. Though it appeared to be a solution to Elkanah's problem, marrying a second wife would only remind Hannah of her struggle with barrenness.

The dream she nurtured since adolescence of blossoming into a young lady, going through a special courtship and marriage, had come to pass. Unfortunately, plans of having a child, nursing a baby, rocking him to sleep and making special clothes seemed to be slipping from her grasp.

Finding her Cause

Dr. LeRoy Gruner, a professor of Sociology at several Ivy League universities and a colleague of mine, has traveled the world studying group behavior for over 40 years. He has been instrumental in establishing Teen Challenge ministries around the world and has dedicated his life to seeing hurting people become healed as they find their true calling in life. In one of our many discussions, I asked him, "Why do some people excel and accomplish goals in their lives, while others quit, fail or don't even try?"

Dr. Gruner answered, "Those who are *accomplishment oriented* are those who have *embraced a cause*. The apex of human development," he continues, "is finding a cause."

Up until now, Hannah's *mission* to have a child has been her *cause*. Now, she begins her journey to battle the doubt that she will never be able to complete her *mission*. According to those around her, she looked like a loser and her hope of becoming a mother was impossible. Many thought she had lost her cause and purpose.

Can you see a different, deflated Hannah? Unable to get pregnant, she is scared and bewildered. She doesn't know why she can't conceive. She's trying to hold it together, even though the future seems gloomy and uncertain. She's been laughed at behind her back, mocked to her face and condemned as a sinner and ostracized. The line is drawn in the sand and she is told to stand on the other side.

Hannah pushes aside her misgivings and worries about her husband. What will the elders think? Who's going to carry on his lineage if she doesn't get pregnant?

She does not want to be a nanny to another woman's child. This was not supposed to happen. This was not the plan.

What about your plans? What about you?

- How has society labeled you and your dreams?
- Are you beginning to believe that the problems you are facing are insurmountable?
- Do you think your goals are out of reach?
- Do you feel like you are losing your grip on the vision that God has put in your heart?

You are not limited by the brand that the world has placed on you. You are defined by the attitude of your heart, your passion and your determination to embrace and fulfill the call God has designed for you. Although rugged, Hannah's journey will begin to reveal the road map to *your* miracle. So let us press on.

CHAPTER 4
A WOMAN MISERABLE

And her rival also provoked her severely, to make her miserable, because the LORD had closed her womb (1 Samuel 1:6).

Even though it was not sanctioned by God, it was customary for a man to take a second wife when his first wife was barren. We can only try to imagine the sense of desolation Hannah must have felt when she learned that Elkanah had finally made the decision to marry a second wife. Her nightmare was now becoming her reality. Her worst fears were coming true.

The new wife's name was Peninnah, which in Hebrew means "Pearl." A precious gem, the pearl is created as a result of irritation and Peninnah did just that!

As Hannah began to grasp the overwhelming reality of her barrenness, she now faced an additional heartache. How would she be treated by her husband's new wife? Every fairy tale has its villain; every Garden of Eden has its snake. What would become of Hannah's fairytale ending?

Can you imagine Hannah and Elkanah's last conversation before he married Peninnah and brought her into their home? I can picture Hannah taking Elkanah's hands, staring lovingly into his eyes with the unspoken question, "Is this woman going to ruin our love for one another and our marriage?" She must have tried to find some sort of comfort in his gaze. I wonder, what did she feel in their last moments together before the new bride moved in?

Hannah looked at her husband, the man of her dreams. The realization that she would now have to share him with another woman flooded her heart. Her eyes glistened with a mixture of tears, uncertainty and unconditional love. In a sweet, soft, quivering voice, did she whisper, "Elkanah, I trust you and I trust God. Please, help me through this transition. My heart is aching. *I want to* believe you when you tell me that everything's going to be alright. I know you said that she will honor and respect me, but how can I be sure I won't lose you?"

I'm sure Elkanah calmly reassured her that everything would be fine. I wonder, did they bow their heads in prayer, submitting their future family to the care of God, or did Hannah merely resign herself to the inevitable? Did she push past the uncertainty and resolve that she would do all that she could to make a happy home for her husband and his new wife? Did she surrender to the anxiety, unsure of what the coming days would hold?

Hannah knew that marriage, like everything worthwhile in life, required dedication, effort and commitment. She understood that even when two people are meant for each other, it was possible for the circumstances of life to challenge their marriage. Would Hannah's inability to conceive drive Elkanah to the temple to ask the rabbi for a divorce?

I'm sure doubt began to creep in. Would their marriage truly last? It seemed like everything was going from bad to worse. She already felt like half a woman, and now he was going to share his life with another wife. Hannah knew she could not afford to entertain these thoughts and let fear control her.

The Two Become Three

As with Hannah and all Hebrew fiancées, Peninnah most likely waited 12 months to marry Elkanah. During Peninnah's time of purification, I'm certain Hannah fervently prayed to God for her miracle baby.

Traditionally, the primary difference between a man's first and subsequent weddings was the noticeable reduction in the number of invited guests, pomp and festivities. As Hannah joined the gathering of family and friends, she wondered if Elkanah and Peninnah were being married under "their" *huppah*.

She didn't know how she was supposed to act when Elkanah took Peninnah inside the *huppah* to consummate their marriage. How did she prepare herself? Even though this *was* a common cultural practice, how would any wife prepare herself for such a thing?

I'm sure Hannah asked God for the fruit of the Spirit, especially self-control to contain her emotions. She must have wondered if this woman was right for Elkanah and if this marriage was the will of God.

As she sat outside the *huppah* with the rest of the wedding party, her heart began to grieve. She became uneasy as sadness and anxiety filled her heart. She watched Elkanah and Peninnah enter the bridal chamber together. The party continued around her, but Hannah did not feel like celebrating.

She sat silently, devastated at the thought of what was taking place inside the *huppah*. After the marriage was consummated, Elkanah announced the good news through the curtain and it spread throughout the wedding party waiting outside. As the word of the marital union reached the town, shouts rang out in the city.

This time there was sadness in Hannah's heart, as well as increasing insecurity and apprehension. She could hear the sound of music and gaiety, but there was no happiness in *her* soul, only uncertainty.

It was an overwhelming, déjà vu experience for Hannah, as her mind quickly replayed, in detail, the cherished memories of her own wedding day. Like last night's dream, Hannah recalled every moment. Everything she felt when both of them floated together, bursting with love and expectation. Now it seemed like a distant memory.

Hannah knew that once the marriage ceremony concluded, Elkanah would be taking Peninnah to their home, the very home she helped create. Would Peninnah enter humbly, or stride across the threshold with an arrogance that announced that this was *her* home and he was *her* man?

How would Peninnah treat her? Would she be friendly and caring, or keep to herself and ignore Hannah? Or even worse, would she treat her with contempt?

If Looks Could Kill

When they all returned home, Hannah stuttered with nervousness, shyly expressing warm compliments as she welcomed Peninnah into the family. To Hannah's surprise, Peninnah's demeanor was cold and distant. She was completely uninterested in befriending Hannah.

Hannah politely excused herself to her designated room allowing the newlyweds to settle in for the night. As she headed toward her room, Hannah quickly glanced at the couple, wanting to make certain that all was prepared for them. As she looked back, her eyes locked briefly with Peninnah's. Hannah's heart was pierced by the harsh stare of her squinted eyes. Then, turning back to her new husband, Peninnah squeezed Elkanah's arm and coyly smiled at him.

Peninnah's glare was a silent snarl, sent like a poisoned arrow that pierced Hannah's heart. Although she was only paralyzed for a split second, it felt like an eternity. It was like a deadly claw had gripped her soul and chills ran down her spine. As she looked back again, Peninnah threw a mocking sneer over her shoulder and confidently waltzed into the bedroom with her new husband.

Hannah was stunned. She lay in bed with her eyes wide open, restless and unable to fall asleep. A spirit of oppression began to burrow its way into her heart. As the long, gloomy night went on, it was filled with waves of discouragement. Hannah fought the memories of the bizarre scene, attempting to convince herself that she had misinterpreted the encounter.

The endless night finally melted away as the sun arose. Hannah waited in her room as long as possible, praying for the strength to be able to treat her new housemate with care and respect. As she walked into the family room, there was Peninnah, reclining in a chair with a self-satisfied smile. Whenever Elkanah turned away, the same snarling gaze returned to Peninnah's face. She looked at Hannah, patting her belly mockingly, as though she had already conceived Elkanah's child.

With the shock of Peninnah's vicious, two-faced actions, the seeds of misery and pain were planted in Hannah's soul. It was in this place that the ground was being prepared for the spirit of bitterness to grow. No matter how hard she tried, each encounter with Peninnah only deepened her pain. Her dream had turned into a nightmare.

Peninnah the Piranha

Peninnah's attacks began as subtle, subversive put-downs, but intensified into vicious assaults, as she attempted to wear Hannah down emotionally and psychologically. The abuse continued and escalated with each passing day, especially when they went to the temple to worship the Lord. Note the Scripture again:

> *And her rival also provoked her severely, to make her miserable, because the LORD had closed her womb. So it was, year by year, when she went up to the house of the LORD, that she provoked her; therefore she wept and did not eat*
>
> (1 Samuel 1:6, 7).

Peninnah increased the intensity of the mocking year by year when they went to the temple. Why the intensity of mocking at the temple? Could it be that Hannah's passion for God in worship and Elkanah's attention intimidated Peninnah? She was determined to discourage Hannah and suck the joy out of her life.

The words "provoked severely" is defined in Hebrew as כעס ka'as *kaw-as'* to trouble; to grieve, rage, be indignant: provoke to anger, sorrow, vexed in spirit.[1]

The Hebrew word "provoked" describes a person who has experienced ongoing mocking, irritation and aggravation, brought on by undeserved mistreatment, which results in sorrow, anger and deep grief.

Peninnah's provocation was a calculated assault on Hannah's mind, heart and mission. It was an attempt to belittle her and crush what little self-esteem remained.

Peninnah's aim was to destroy Hannah's vision. Hannah's adversary attempted to strip her of her identity and question her self-worth. It was part of an evil plan to break her down mentally to the point of making her incapable of executing her duties as a wife.

Today, Peninnah's provoking would be considered bullying. Bullying can be emotionally destructive. The constant mocking, belittling and embarrassment can lead persons to believe that they are worthless and inferior. Bullying inflicts deep wounds of rejection, isolation and can lead people to resort to suicide. Consider this reality: Hannah endured 10-years of bullying, yet held on with hope.

Elkanah's continuing love for Hannah fueled Peninnah's envy and jealousy. It made her a daily target of contempt and ridicule. Instead of bonding as a family and bringing offerings to God, Peninnah chose to deliberately mock Hannah. She constantly reminded Hannah of her barrenness by belittling her. Peninnah sowed seeds of dissension and strife rather than honoring and worshipping God.

The pain of seeing her beloved with this deceitful woman was overwhelming. When she heard that Peninnah was carrying Elkanah's first child, the anguish was more than she could bear. The thought of her nursing Elkanah's child created an ache she could hardly endure.

Hannah's home, which should have been a place of security, comfort and peace, became a battleground. The vicious assaults and ongoing attacks began to take their toll.

Battleground in the Home

As Passover drew near, Hannah tried to console herself in faith, not giving up on her desire to have a child. After all, *if* Peninnah's first child was a girl, perhaps the following year Hannah would be the one to carry her beloved's *male heir* to the celebration. Unfortunately, this was not the case. Year after year, Peninnah bore Elkanah sons and daughters.

Let us pause for a moment and think about the constant disappointment

Hannah had to face. *Desperate* to get pregnant, each month presented a *significant opportunity* for her dream to come true. However, as each month passed, the stigma of infertility was reinforced again.

We know that Peninnah bore sons and daughters, which means she must have had at least four or more children during what Bible commentators estimate could be a 10 year period. This means Hannah's hopes of conceiving a child were dashed 12 times a year with a total of more than 120 deep disappointments. Over 120 times, Hannah held her breath in anticipation, only to exhale unfulfilled expectations.

Nothing seemed to satisfy Peninnah. Even though she had children, the heir to carry on the family name and the attention of Elkanah, it was still not enough. As long as there was a connection between Elkanah and Hannah, Peninnah was determined to humiliate Hannah. She would continue until Hannah was forced out of the family or suffered an emotional breakdown. Peninnah was driven to have Elkanah all to herself.

The Olive Press

I would not presume to compare Hannah's misery with the suffering of our Savior, but the expressive words that describe her suffering parallel the experience of Jesus in the Garden of Gethsemane. On the night before His crucifixion, He went to Gethsemane to pray. While He was there, He experienced excruciating emotional torment.

How relevant is the fact that the name Gethsemane means "olive press." Like Jesus and like Hannah, we will all go through times when we're going to experience the "olive press of life." There will be seasons when we will feel the weight of suffering, discouragement and hopelessness that comes upon us. It can deter us, destroy us or it can make us more determined. If we allow Him to, God can use it to prepare us for the calling He has placed on our lives.

When a person goes through a "Gethsemane" experience, it's always a painful struggle; but as we drink from the cup of suffering, we mature and grow into all that God wants us to be. If we truly desire to be people of godly character and are willing to embrace the process, it is critical to have a revelation of what Jesus went through in the Garden of Gethsemane. Three of the Gospels describe the emotional, mental and physical trauma that Jesus endured.

Then He said to them, 'My soul is <u>exceedingly sorrowful,</u> even to death
(Matthew 26:38).

And being in <u>agony,</u> He prayed more earnestly. Then His sweat became like great drops of blood falling down to the ground (Luke 22:44).

He said to His disciples, 'Sit here while I pray'…and He began to be <u>troubled</u> and <u>deeply distressed</u> (Mark 14:32, 33).

To get a better understanding of what Jesus endured in Gethsemane, I have defined the underlined expressions documented by the disciples. As we look at these words, it gives us a picture of the olive press encounter. We will also see these similar expressions from Hannah as she defined her own condition.

- Sorrow: <u>Greek:</u> "lupe" - sadness, heaviness, mourning with fear and dread, to render anxious or distressed, to perplex the mind.
- Agony: <u>Greek:</u> "agonia" - to tremble, to travail, a severe mental and emotional struggle for victory.
- Troubled: <u>Greek:</u> "tarasso" - to agitate, to cause one inward commotion, to strike one's spirit with fear and dread, to render anxious or distressed, to perplex the mind.
- Distress: <u>Greek:</u> "stenochoria" - narrowness of place, dire calamity, extreme affliction.[2]

The words, *sorrow, agony, troubled* and *distress,* express an all-encompassing pain that deeply traumatized Jesus' entire being, causing emotional convulsions throughout the body, mind and spirit. The anguish was so deep that it caused His blood vessels on His brow to burst and "His sweat became like great drops of blood" (Luke 22:44).

I have shared that Jesus' physical body died on the cross, but He first died to "self," and surrendered to the Father's will, in the Garden of Gethsemane. It was then that He declared, "Not My will, but Yours, be done" (Luke 22:42).

The years of abuse that Hannah endured at the hands of Peninnah and the town's people resulted in the misery that was undoubtedly *her* Gethsemane. The painful journey was a critical part of the character development of this godly woman. Hannah was being tested and purified through seemingly impossible circumstances. Her character was being sculpted through these trials. When her friends, family and even her own expectations came against her, she looked to

God for her strength and perseverance the same way Jesus did in the Garden.

The Bible expresses the pain Hannah held in her heart and the misery she resolutely endured through the words of Samuel 1.

Her rival also <u>provoked</u> her severely, to make her <u>miserable</u>, because the LORD *had closed her womb* (1 Samuel 1:6).

Hannah, why do you weep? Why do you not eat? And why is your heart <u>grieved</u>?
(1 Samuel 1:8).

And she was in <u>bitterness</u> of soul and prayed to the LORD *and wept in <u>anguish</u>*
(1 Samuel 1:10).

O LORD *of hosts, if You will indeed look on the <u>affliction</u> of Your maidservant and remember me…*(1 Samuel 1:11).

No, my lord, I am a woman of <u>sorrowful</u> spirit (1 Samuel 1:15).

When we combine each of these seven afflictions that Hannah experienced, they create the inner olive press that she too endured.

Let's look into these words in the Hebrew as they define the hardship she experienced.

- **Provoked:** <u>Hebrew</u>: "ka'as" - to trouble; to grieve, rage, be indignant: provoke to anger, sorrow, vexed in spirit.
- **Misery:** <u>Hebrew</u>: "ra` am" - to be violently agitated; to crash of thunder, to irritate with anger. To cause to tremble, to trouble, worry of body and mind; grievance, pain, sorrow, toil, travail, trouble, wearisome.
- **Grieved:** <u>Hebrew</u>: "ya-ra" - to be broken up with violent action, to fear, to tremble, to quiver.
- **Bitterness:** <u>Hebrew</u>: "marah" - painful anger, chafed, discontented, wickedness.
- **Anguish:** <u>Hebrew</u>: "bakah" - to weep; generally to bemoan, bewail, make lamentation, mourn with tears.
- **Affliction:** <u>Hebrew</u>: "`anah" - looking down or browbeating; to depress, chasten, deal hardly with, hurt, ravish, to be busied with, to be depressed, to be downcast.
- **Sorrowful:** <u>Hebrew</u>: "qashen" - grievous, fierce, intense, vehement, miserable. [3]

In the verses above, the painful expressions recorded in the Bible provide clear insight into Hannah's broken heart. Provocation, misery, grief, bitterness, anguish, affliction and a sorrowful spirit are all ingredients that could have destroyed her dream. Like Jesus, Hannah was carrying a huge burden of emotional pain. As she expressed these emotions, they became more than just words. The weight was overwhelming. She could have easily surrendered her dream in despair rather than fight for her miracle.

As she faced constant provocation, it appeared that Peninnah was succeeding in her evil goal. It seemed that she might have actually derailed the vision God had given Hannah for her life. The seeds that Peninnah had planted were beginning to grow and were in danger of choking out her dreams.

Shattered Dream

Have you ever experienced a shattered dream? I've been there and I know firsthand what it feels like to live with failed dreams. In my book, *I Can Dream Again - The Jimmy Jack Story*, I give a detailed account of my mother's story, which had a tremendous impact on my life and my dreams.

Immediately after my parents' honeymoon, World War II broke out and my father enlisted in the Army. Right away, my mother was left alone, not knowing what would become of her husband. Her worst fears would be realized sometime later, when she received a letter stating that my father had been shot down over Germany and was MIA (Missing in Action). She was left to wonder if the man she loved was dead or alive.

If he was alive, what was he enduring? She later learned that he had been captured and had been taken to a prisoner-of-war camp where he faced much abuse and torment. Although my father returned home, the mental and emotional damage was done, which would affect him later in life.

When he returned, he became a football Hall of Famer for Cortland University. He was also the first athletic director for the largest school district on Long Island, overseeing 23 schools. However, from there things went terribly wrong. Because of his experience in the concentration camp, he held an explosive cargo of deep pain in his soul. Later in life, that cargo would implode and affect our entire family.

The white community's rejection of our family, coupled with my father's distress, left all of us afflicted, anguished and angry. The seeds of bitterness that were sown now flourished into destructive lifestyles.

Social rejection caused deep wounds in all of my siblings' hearts. That rejection developed into a survival mentality which manifested as rebellion against authority and society. This was an attempt to create self-esteem and social acceptance. It became a part of our everyday life, as we escaped through drug and alcohol abuse that led to crimes against society.

Hannah endured years of abuse. Hell was determined to destroy God's plan for Hannah through the seeds of hatred that Peninnah planted in her heart. Those seeds began to produce weeds of bitterness in her soul.

Hidden Cargo

The causes of bitterness may vary, but all have the same result. Bitterness is an explosive, hidden cargo that sabotages one's destiny.

I'm reminded of the wartime attack on the passenger liner, the *Lusitania*. This tragic story parallels the deadly reality of the consequences of carrying bitterness in our heart.

When the *Lusitania* was built in 1907, the owners wanted to construct the fastest passenger ship in the world. To all who saw the *Lusitania*, she appeared to be a safe, luxurious ocean liner. However, on a fateful trip from the United States to England, an illegal cargo, hidden in the hold, would lead to a catastrophe.

The start of the First World War in 1914 made the open seas dangerous for passenger ships like the *Lusitania*. Many ocean-going vessels became the unintended casualties of this war. The *Lusitania* began its fateful voyage on May 1, 1915, sailing from New York to Liverpool, England.

Everyone recognized the dangers of submarine attacks in those contested Atlantic waterways. With famous world leaders and the wealthiest of the ruling class on board, the company was confident that crossing the battle-torn waterways on the 32,000-ton *Lusitania* would be safe.

The *Lusitania* sailed across the Atlantic and boldly steamed into the war zone on the morning of May 7, 1915. At the same time, the British Navy was alerted to the presence of a German submarine in the waters along the southern part of the Irish Channel. It had already sunk three ships. Knowing that the *Lusitania* was on her way to Liverpool, officials issued a warning:

> *Submarine active in southern part of Irish Channel. Last heard of twenty miles south of Conningbeg light vessel. Make certain Lusitania gets this.*[4]

For safety purposes, William Turner, the captain of the *Lusitania*, was

MISERABLE

directed to detour and make port at Queenstown, instead of continuing to Liverpool. Unfortunately, that instruction brought them *directly* in line with the enemy submarine.

As the *Lusitania* deviated from its course, the German sub caught sight of her and fired a torpedo. The torpedo struck the ship like a giant hammer, slamming into its steel hull. Immediately afterward, a much larger *second* explosion tore a huge hole in the keel, damaging it severely. It took only 18 minutes for the *Lusitania* to sink to the bottom of the ocean, along with its 1,119 passengers.[5]

We know the German torpedo caused the *first* explosion. However, the logbook from the German sub does not record launching a second torpedo, so what was the cause of the *second* explosion? Was there something concealed deep in the bowels of *Lusitania's* cargo hold?

The Germans alleged that there were weapons secretly hidden in the ship. According to the ship's manifest, the *Lusitania* carried its normal load of food and beverages. However, German authorities suspected that where the manifest listed an enormous amount of "cheese," there were actually tens of thousands of tons of weapons and explosives. Since the *Lusitania* did not have a refrigerated cargo system, it would have been impossible for her to transport cheese.

Under maritime law, it has *always* been illegal to transport munitions, weapons or explosives as cargo on a passenger vessel. While on the surface, everything appeared to be legal, *the deadly secret below was 51 tons of three-inch shells, six million bullets and 200 tons of ammunition.*[6]

On December 19, 2008, divers discovered those munitions in the cargo compartment 300 feet below the water's surface. It is clear that it was *not* just the torpedo that sank the *Lusitania*, but the explosive payload beneath the water line. The "hidden things," her illegal cargo, caused her demise. Even though the ship was built strong enough to handle the impact of a torpedo, the vessel could not withstand an explosion from deep within the bowels of the ship.

In the same way, the dangerous payload of bitterness is *unlawful cargo* for a child of God. It is the root cause of many *shipwrecks* of faith. Most often, bitterness arises from circumstances and relationships. It can lead to antagonism, hostility and cynicism. The situations that were causing Hannah's misery made her vulnerable to bitterness.

Here is the way bitterness develops. God gives us the strength to handle the daily struggles and disappointments that we face. *But,* if we allow disappointments to turn into misery, then misery turns into bitterness. Rather than giving our wounds to God, we begin to store up a *payload* of bitterness within the depths of our soul. Before long we are filled with hazardous, combustible baggage. Then one day, one of life's little torpedoes hits that cargo compartment in your soul and an explosion occurs.

In the sinking of the *Lusitania*, we see the unintended consequences of carrying hidden payload. In the life of Hannah, we see God's protection. Hebrews warns us of the dangers of carrying the illegal cargo of bitterness.

Pursue peace with all people and holiness, without which no one will see the Lord: looking carefully lest anyone fall short of the grace of God; lest any root of bitterness springing up cause trouble and by this many become defiled (Hebrews 12:14, 15).

This biblical reference serves as a warning from God on how this deadly stronghold infects the soul. Bitterness imprisons your heart and blocks God's grace. Grace is God's unmerited favor. Grace opens the door for forgiveness, whereas bitterness locks the door of grace. A bitter heart refuses to forgive and is unable to receive forgiveness.

Bitterness results in a critical spirit that finds something wrong in every situation. When you are bitter, even when God bestows a blessing on your life, you will not be able to enjoy its fullness and may even see it as a problem. Bitterness is a blockade to gratefulness, peace and the appreciation of everyday life. False expectations lead to disappointment, which only feeds the bitterness.

When we unload the explosive cargo, we find the truth about bitterness. Misery fosters bitterness and bitterness can take hold of your life. Left unchecked, it grows and becomes a major stronghold. It locks us in and locks everyone else out. While a stronghold may keep earthly enemies out, its greatest danger is blocking what God wants to do in our lives.

It took a toll on Hannah's relationship with her husband, as well as her overall happiness. It had the potential of destroying her dreams, but she had a decision to make. She could either believe the lies, or believe the truth that God placed in her heart. In spite of the attacks of the enemy to make her miserable, Hannah stood strong.

I heard Brother David Wilkerson say, "It is impossible to be wrong with man and right with God at the same time." In other words, you cannot be bitter toward people and feel that you're walking in a right relationship with

God. Bitterness causes you to walk in the flesh and not in the Spirit. It is a by-product of unforgiveness and results in spiritual death.

- Has your misery grown into bitterness?
- Is bitterness blocking the conception of your dreams?
- Is there someone in your life that you need to forgive?
- Are you harboring bitterness toward someone?

Let all bitterness, wrath, anger, clamor and evil speaking be put away from you, with all malice. And be kind to one another, tenderhearted, forgiving one another, even as God in Christ forgave you (Ephesians 4:31, 32).

Thankfully, love and forgiveness are God's eternal antidotes to this toxic stronghold. Hannah remained firm in her belief that God loved her and had not abandoned her, even when it appeared that others had.

- Bitterness sours life. Love and forgiveness sweeten life.
- Bitterness sickens life. Love and forgiveness heal life.
- Bitterness blinds life. Love and forgiveness enlighten life.
- Bitterness paralyzes. Love and forgiveness empower life.
- Bitterness imprisons. Love and forgiveness release life.

Even when someone causes you great pain and harm, remember that bitterness will destroy you and hurt those who love you. Therefore, forgive those who hurt you. Surrender your bitterness and your pain to the Lord and let Him set you free. Get rid of your combustible cargo before a small spark triggers a huge explosion!

CHAPTER 5
MISUNDERSTOOD

Then Elkanah her husband said to her, 'Hannah, why do you weep? Why do you not eat? And why is your heart grieved? Am I not better to you than ten sons?'
(1 Samuel 1:8).

We cannot help but feel Hannah's emotional trauma. We identify with her pain as she endured the torment of being a woman marked, miserable and a victim on Peninnah's hit list. Now add to this heartbreak, the pain of being misunderstood. Nothing says *clueless* like her husband's pompous response, "Am I not better to you than ten sons?"

Whispers Behind Her Back

In the childless years that followed her marriage to Elkanah, the despondency of grief, insecurity and low self-esteem took their toll. Her days of walking with a cheerful stride, assurance and expectation had vanished. As she shopped in the marketplace, her countenance was downcast. It wasn't her food basket that was weighing her down; it was her burdens.

The air of confidence was gone. Though at one time she had been esteemed and envied, she was now followed by mocking whispers. Carrying the burden of barrenness, she still tried to hold onto her vision of motherhood.

Her peers, especially those who once coveted her blessings, snickered in self-satisfied scorn. No matter how careful they were to hide their whispers, she could read their body language as they scoffed. She wondered, were they saying, "Ha! There's Hannah, the barren woman. Look, where is her swagger now?"

Others patronized her with empty words of consolation, but she could see in their eyes a spirit of superiority and pity. They did not even try to hide their judgment. To many around her, she was an infertile, failure of a woman. God must be punishing her for some hidden sin, for she was clearly never going to be a mother. Even though *they* looked upon her as cursed, and at times she *felt* cursed, she refused to believe the lie.

Her vision and reality collided on the tracks of confusion. She felt like everyone misunderstood her. Compounding her plight, it seemed like Peninnah always had the upper hand. Her adversary, her afflicter, her provoker now dominated *Hannah's home* with *Hannah's man*.

For Hannah, this was not just paranoia or feeling sorry for herself. First Samuel makes it clear that the circumstances around her were becoming increasingly unbearable.

And her rival also provoked her severely, to make her miserable, because the Lord had closed her womb. So it was, year by year, when she went up to the house of the Lord, that she provoked her; therefore she wept and did not eat

(1 Samuel 1:6, 7).

Like Hannah, my mother was also provoked severely by those who were close to her. As my brothers and sisters grew older and our lives continued to fall apart, most of us cursed my mother, blaming her for all of our problems. During those painful years, they often told her that she had sacrificed our family for her cause.

My mother endured dishonor, disrespect and constant attacks on her life. She went against the norms of society and stood up against prejudice, social injustice and discrimination. Not only did our neighbors and relatives misunderstand and mock my mother's mission; her own children misunderstood her as well.

The family began to deteriorate and so did my mother's mental health. As the abuse from the community escalated, my mother's mission to bring about change threatened to destroy our entire family. Just like everyone was trying to derail my mother's dream, Peninnah's goal was to destroy Hannah's dream as well.

He's Just Clueless

At a time when Hannah was at the edge of defeat, walking through the valley of despair, what she needed most was support and understanding. Her husband and pastor, two of the most significant people in her life, totally let her down.

First, her husband trivialized her needs. When Elkanah observed Hannah weeping and fasting, his response was cold and insensitive. He knew she was still holding onto her dream. His response was likely an effort to help her get hold of reality. That is a typical male response, but to Hannah it just confirmed that no one understood her or believed in her vision.

Then Elkanah her husband said to her, 'Hannah, why do you weep? Why do you not eat? And why is your heart grieved? Am I not better to you than ten sons?'

(1 Samuel 1:8).

His words, meant to comfort, pierced like an arrow right through her soul. Elkanah's lofty opinion of himself cut through her wall of protection, wounding her more deeply than even the murmuring of the city gossips. While his macho man response, "Oh baby, I am all you need," felt good to him, he totally missed it. He was oblivious to his wife's emotional needs. He left her feeling empty and isolated, holding onto the impossible dream of motherhood all alone.

I can see her wearied body shudder at Elkanah's insensitive response. Slowly turning in submissive obedience, she dried her tears as the desire to retaliate tried to rise. His words only intensified the pain that seeped from her grieving heart. You may have felt the sting of insensitive, well-meaning but misplaced comfort, but don't despair. That was not the end of her story.

All that remained were the nagging doubts that she had to fight off. Could she have been deceived by her own mind? Was her belief that God had a plan to give her a child just a *product of her own imagination*? That would be the cruelest irony of it all!

If there was ever a time Hannah needed strength and power from the Holy Spirit to secure her heart, it was now. Hannah stood in the midst of being provoked, mocked and misunderstood.

With every ounce of grace within her, somehow she contained herself and gave no reply. Heaven's hand was upon her. It had to be God's strength that filled her heart with self-control in the face of her husband's response. This woman of grace had held her complaint for *years*. This was a testimony of her inner resolve to fulfill the vision that she believed God had for her life.

Get Over It!

Let me pause for a moment. If you are a woman reading this book, you may have already nodded your head in full understanding because you have felt Hannah's pain, or shaken your head in disappointment at her husband's words. Elkanah's response revealed his heart. The Bible tells us, "For out of the abundance of the heart his mouth speaks" (Luke 6:45). He just wasn't getting it.

As a man, allow me to admit that Elkanah's reaction was selfish and insensitive because men have a tendency to act, not feel. Men are always looking for a quick solution.

Perhaps his response grew out of frustration. He finally revealed his true feelings about Hannah's inability to accept *her reality*. He just wanted her to move on. It was obvious to him that holding onto her dream was causing her so much pain. Why not just get over it?

Some people think you can turn emotions and expectations on and off. Unfortunately, feelings are not just a switch that you can flip to make the pain go away.

At the very time when Hannah needed reassurance, comfort and understanding, Elkanah was not there for her. In his impatience, he told her to be content with her life. "This is the hand you were dealt, Baby. Get a grip, face reality and perform your wifely duties. Accept the fact that you will never have a child and that you are blessed just to have *me*!"

Elkanah's response was merely arrogance coated in ignorance. He completely misunderstood Hannah's dream to have a child. His insensitivity hurt her along with his attitude of condescending superiority. As he expressed his disappointment and questioned her for weeping, he demonstrated his inability to understand her tears, prayers and vision.

Elkanah was so focused on how her dreams inconvenienced him, that he overlooked her passion for motherhood, her emotional stress and weariness of soul.

He was oblivious to the mocking, insults and especially the vicious, verbal claws of Peninnah. Consequently, Elkanah's ignorance felt like just another assault, one more source of pain.

Missing the Mark

I will admit that sometimes I have fallen short of discernment and have misunderstood my wife, Miriam. For example, on the night before I was going away to start writing this book, Miriam wanted to spend some quality time together. She became frustrated when I invited a few friends from church to come over to watch a football game.

On this particular night, the New York Jets were playing their rival, the New England Patriots, in the AFC Championship Game. Miriam tried to convince me *not* to have company over, especially since they had been there the previous Sunday. But to me, there was nothing wrong.

Allow me to plead my case. The Jets hadn't been in the Super Bowl since Joe Namath led them to victory in 1969, in one of the greatest upsets in sports history. I invited the boys over because I had a new, large flat screen TV.

Now, I did have a romantic plan for Miriam that evening. I figured after the game ended, at about 9 p.m., we could spend the rest of the night together. However, my plans changed when additional Jets fans unexpectedly showed up. Miriam, the thoughtful wife that she is, made sure we had our chicken wings, chips and soda prior to retreating to her friend's house for a break.

The Jets won! We were all ecstatic. Eventually everyone left. When Miriam came home, *I* was ready for some *quality time*, but *she* was tired and upset with me. Our *quality time*, ended up in *quarrel time* and *lesson time* for me. I missed *the moment* that night.

Here is where I went wrong. When I told Miriam I was going to have a couple of fellows over, she asked me not to. Her concern was that she didn't want to have to rush home from church to clean the house, prepare food and everything else that comes along with inviting guests.

I told Miriam not to worry. *I* would get the food and clean up the house and s*he* would not have to do anything. So she gave in. I've been with Miriam for over 30 years. I should know by now that it's impossible for her to do *nothing*.

The mind of a man tends to experience convenient amnesia when it benefits him. It was not until *after* the night ended...*after* I rushed to pack my suitcases and gather my studying and writing resources...and *after* I had left the house at 3:30 a.m. to catch my 6 a.m. flight, that I began to consider *her needs*. I got the revelation at 30,000 feet, "high-sight," while on the plane. I finally got it, at least on this one particular issue.

I needed to see past her words about cooking and cleaning to hear her *actual* need. Miriam wanted to be alone with me that evening. She wanted to spend quality time, have dinner together, relax and help me get ready for my early flight. Even if I had gone over to watch the game at someone else's house, it would have been fine. Miriam could have relaxed at home and prepared our nest for us to enjoy the rest of the evening together.

I thought, *I blew it again*! On the plane I began to think, *Why do men get discernment after the fact?"* Hindsight is 20/20 for most men when it comes to women. Women often *get it* before the fact. I got it at 30,000 feet.

Love and Understanding

Husbands tend to be preoccupied with *their world*, distracted by *their drive* and *their goals*. They think that women think the way they think. As a consequence, we try to satisfy our wives needs based on what satisfies us. Left to our own selfishness, men miss the fact that our wives often feel neglected, lonely and misunderstood. So it comes as no surprise to me that Elkanah totally missed the mark with Hannah.

Over the years, through hundreds of counseling sessions and countless hours ministering to couples, the statement I hear most often is, "He doesn't listen to me. He doesn't understand me."

Miriam has said these same things to me, so I completely relate to the husband's inability to understand the needs of his wife. While writing this book and engaging in study and prayer, I realized my own weakness in this area.

I asked God to unclog my spiritual ears and tenderize my heart. I want to be sensitive to Miriam's needs; to honor, understand and love her, the way *she needs* to be loved. This will involve listening to her and honoring and respecting her as the wife, mother, ministry leader and woman of God that she is.

This task may seem simple, but for a man to actually fulfill these needs will require a deep desire to understand what makes a woman secure. I think like a man, talk like a man, walk like a man, smell like a man and react like a man. I need to take the necessary time and effort to understand Miriam's reality. It may seem like a task of tremendous undertaking, but with God's help, it is possible.

How to Satisfy a Woman

Some time ago when I was at a carpet warehouse in the men's bathroom, I noticed a scroll hanging on the wall. It was six feet long and stated in large print, *"How to Satisfy a Woman/How to Satisfy a Man."* The illustration began with a list of women's needs…

Caress, praise, pamper, relish, savor, massage, make plans, fix, empathize, serenade, compliment, support, feed, tantalize, humor, placate, console, hug, cuddle, excite, pacify, protect, correspond, anticipate, nuzzle, smooch and, of course, get hair and nails done and go shopping, etc. The list on the scroll went on for five and a half feet with a hundred different ways describing the needs of women. It concluded, "Do this and you will satisfy your woman."

I could not help but chuckle as I continued reading. At the bottom of the scroll it said, *"How to Satisfy a Man."* As I read on, I thought, *This should be interesting.* One short sentence read, "Give him a little romance and some food!" I laughed and I got the point. Men's and women's needs are *completely* different.

I see more and more the importance of listening, and more important than that, hearing. After speaking at a church in England, the pastor took me out to lunch. We got into a conversation about listening to the voice of God. He shared with me an illustration on how he learned to become sensitive to God's voice through listening to the voice of his wife.

He told me about the time when his wife was hospitalized and had to undergo a tracheotomy. While removing the tubes from her throat, the doctors injured her vocal chords and permanently damaged her voice. When she talked it was a raspy whisper. He shared, "I had to learn to hear her voice all over again."

In an effort to demonstrate how he listens to her, he moved in closer to me. In a soft whisper he said, "Pastor Jimmy, I've learned to hear my wife's voice from across the room with 50 people talking." I sat there in awe. Tears welled up and since then one of my prayers has been, "God, please help me to really hear my wife's voice and the voice of the Holy Spirit."

Men assume that what satisfies them satisfies women. The bottom level of the pyramid of human development is meeting our physiological needs. These needs include food, clothing, shelter and sex. Now, these needs may satisfy a simple man, but not a virtuous woman like my wife, Miriam, or a woman like Hannah.

Misunderstood by Her Priest

Where did Hannah go after the insensitive words of her husband? She turned to her one haven: her church, the temple, the place where she could worship God and unveil her heart. Unfortunately, she found no acceptance there either. Instead, she endured another painful attack from her spiritual leader.

"Pastor" Eli, the high priest, chastised Hannah while she was in prayer at the temple and accused her of being drunk. Eli did not recognize her true heart cry and demeaned her for weeping, as she prayed for God to grant her heart's desire.

> *So Hannah arose after they had finished eating and drinking in Shiloh. Now Eli the priest was sitting on the seat by the doorpost of the tabernacle of the LORD. And she was in bitterness of soul and prayed to the LORD and wept in anguish*
> (1 Samuel 1:9, 10).

And it happened, as she continued praying before the LORD, that Eli watched her mouth. Now Hannah spoke in her heart; only her lips moved, but her voice was not heard. Therefore Eli thought she was drunk. So Eli said to her, 'How long will you be drunk? Put your wine away from you!'
(1 Samuel 1:9, 12-14).

Don't miss this moment! She is on her knees in deep intercession, pouring out her heart to the Lord. As if she had not already been mocked and misunderstood, the Bible gives us a detailed description of the final indignity. In the most sacred place, in the most sincere spiritual condition, in the presence of God, Hannah is rebuked by her pastor. He saw her lips moving, but did not hear what she was praying. He carelessly concluded she was drunk.

Can you imagine? Hannah is in an intense emotional and spiritual state. Suddenly, as she is seeking God, she is jolted from her solitude, interrupted by the harsh accusation of Eli, "How long will you be drunk? Put your wine away from you!" (1 Samuel 1:14).

Once again, Hannah displayed her character by responding to this unjust indictment in humility and reverence.

But Hannah answered and said, 'No, my lord, I am a woman of sorrowful spirit. I have drunk neither wine nor intoxicating drink, but have poured out my soul before the LORD. Do not consider your maidservant a wicked woman, for out of the abundance of my complaint and grief I have spoken until now'
(1 Samuel 1:15, 16).

Every time I read this passage and read Eli's insulting words, my spirit shakes and my heart feels her grief. Then, in her defense, I want to jump into the scene and fight her battle, but I'm quickly relieved to know that her faith and favor sustained her and caused her to prevail.

Closed for a Divine Time

The LORD had closed her womb (1 Samuel 1:5).

There are many reasons why women are unable to conceive. Medical science reveals a multitude of systemic issues from hormonal problems, to failure to produce mature eggs, or malfunction of the fallopian tubes. There are also other physical and emotional roots that can prevent a woman from having a baby.

In research published in the *Journal of Human Reproduction*, doctors compared pregnancy rates in couples that reported being stressed and those who were not. They found that pregnancy was much more likely to occur during months when couples reported feeling happy and relaxed. It was less likely to occur during the months they reported feeling tense or anxious.[1]

Not only does stress hinder the reproductive system, but steals one's joy and optimism and an oppressive spirit sets in. Hannah had to fight off the claws of depression with every ounce of faith she had. This was an additional burden that must have weighed her down physically with every step she took toward her vision.

In Hannah's case, it is not as important to identify a biological explanation for her infertility as the fact that the Bible says that "God had closed her womb." I believe Hannah had a revelation that her barrenness was more than just a biological issue.

While other people cast accusation and condemnation that God closed her womb to punish her, she saw only God's purpose. She consoled herself that if God had been the One to close her womb, then He would be the One to open her womb.

Hannah's testimony speaks to us all. The truth is that there are times in our lives that God will close a door. Do not despair. Even if, *in His infinite wisdom,* God chooses to close a door, He can open that door again or unlock another door. But, *before* God opens a closed door, He opens our *heart* and *eyes* to His purpose. Doors open only when we arise in faith like Hannah, allowing God to remove inner strongholds and move forward. Doors will open in the process of time, when we allow God to do a new thing in our lives.

This truth is clearly reflected in the Book of Revelation.

These things says He who is holy, He who is true, 'He who has the key of David, He who opens and no one shuts and shuts and no one opens.' 'I know your works. See, I have set before you an open door and no one can shut it; for you have a little strength, have kept My word and have not denied My name' (Revelation 3:7, 8).

God at times will keep the door to your miracle closed until you allow Him to dig deep and build a foundation that can support the weight of the blessing He is about to bring into your life. The proving of your faith during the testing period will protect you, so that when you go through the door of your miracle, you will have the wisdom, understanding and godly character to maintain the blessing and not make an idol out of it.

I have learned that faith that has not been tested is faith that cannot be trusted. Hannah's faith was tested year after year, so God knew she could be trusted.

In Revelation, God declares,

For you have a little strength, [you] have kept My word and have not denied My name (Revelation 3:8).

We must fulfill what God requires in Revelation, as Hannah did, in order for our miracles to manifest. She faced every trial, even in her weakest moments, with the little strength she had left. Hannah kept God's Word and did not deny His name.

God is always faithful to His promises to those who love, fear, believe and trust Him.

But without faith it is impossible to please Him, for he who comes to God must believe that He is and that He is a rewarder of those who diligently seek Him
(Hebrews 11:6).

Remember, your gift will take you to the open door. Your faith and obedience will take you through the door and character will keep you there.

Never lose sight of the fact that the *blessing* is not *the promise*. The true blessing is *the One who promised it*. In order to allow God to do a new thing in your life and open a new door to your destiny, deep change is required because God's ways are not our ways. In God's immeasurable knowledge and divine providence, He always has a higher and greater plan in mind.

'For My thoughts are not your thoughts, nor are your ways My ways,' says the LORD. 'For as the heavens are higher than the earth, so are My ways higher than your ways and My thoughts than your thoughts' (Isaiah 55:8, 9).

My friend Mark Batterson, author of *The Circle Maker,* gives a wonderful, thought-provoking, numerical perspective on the unlimited height of God's ways in Isaiah 55.

The sun is the nearest star in our tiny little galaxy known as the Milky Way. There are more than 80 billion galaxies in the universe, which, for the record, equates to more than 10 galaxies per person! I don't think you have to worry about running out of things to do when you get to heaven. It's an awfully big sandbox.

In one minute, light travels 11 million miles. In one day, light travels 160 billion miles. In one year, light- travels an unfathomable 5 trillion, 865 billion, 696 million miles. But that's just one light-year. The outer edge of the universe, according to astrophysicists, is 15.5 billion light-years away! If that seems incomprehensible, it's because it's virtually unimaginable. Yet God says that this is the distance between His thoughts and our thoughts.

So here's my thought: Your best thought on your best day falls 15.5 billion light-years short of how great and how good God really is. Even the most brilliant among us underestimate God by 15.5 billion light years. God is able to do 15.5 billion light-years beyond what you can ask or imagine.²

As expansive as the heavenlies are, we must realize it is impossible to fathom God's ways with our finite minds. When we fully yield to His will and miraculous destiny for our lives, the vision we presently have is minute compared to God's vision for us. As the Bible declares…

Now to Him who is able to do <u>exceedingly</u> <u>abundantly</u> above all that we ask or think, according to the power that works in us
                                                                              (Ephesians 3:20).

As much as *you* want to plan your life, God has a way of surprising you with unexpected blessings that bring you more joy than you could have imagined. Your understanding must be transformed and aligned with God's desires for your life.

The three C's in life are choices, chances and changes. You must make the choice, to take the chance if you want anything to change. Change doesn't come easy, as is evident with Hannah's story. Even though it can be very painful, it is worth the cost. *Change flows from a humble heart, yielded to God.*

Pain Is Temporary. Quitting Lasts Forever.

I have experienced many trials in the ministry. I have carried burdens to provide for the physical, spiritual and financial needs for over 200 ladies and men in our Teen Challenge residential houses. There are also multitudes of at-risk children, teens and families that we touch through our outreaches. But that is not the hardest part.

I have experienced emotional, physical and spiritual attacks on my family and have been betrayed. One of the heaviest burdens I've encountered was the pain of betrayal when people I have sacrificed for, poured my life into and trusted, have unexpectedly turned on me.

It's at these times when relationships are broken, you feel empty and abandoned. All of us will experience times of loneliness, but some people live in it for years. Hannah understood what it meant to feel all alone. Being misunderstood is a very lonely place. From the first day she encountered Peninnah's vindictive stare, a spirit of rejection tried to creep into Hannah's being. It was Peninnah's desire driven by hell's fury to divide and destroy the family.

The sense of being constantly misunderstood also brings a feeling of rejection. Rejection produces a wounded, insecure heart. That wounded heart becomes further infected with loneliness. Loneliness leads to isolation and isolation produces a resistant heart. Proverbs 18:1 says, "A man who isolates himself seeks his own desire; He rages against all wise judgment."

Being misunderstood, lonely, rejected and isolated separates you from one of the most important God-ordained human needs: belongingness. As I mentioned, the apex of human development is having a cause. Belongingness is a vital need.

If we could see our lives as a pyramid, the wide base level represents our physiological needs. There are six levels in the progression leading to the apex (peak) of the pyramid which is our self actualization (cause). At the center of these levels of human development is the third level of "belongingness."[3]

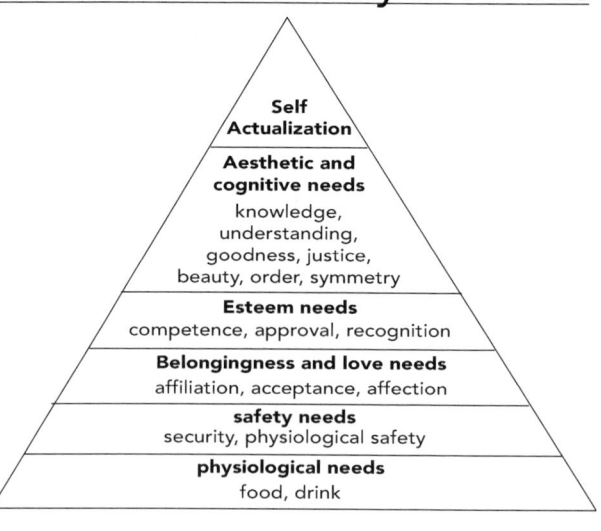

Belongingness is the state of development related to a person's desire to feel important, needed, recognized, affirmed, appreciated, listened to and loved. Yes, we all need belongingness, a sense of purpose and a cause!

Double-Edged Sword

Loneliness is a strange dichotomy. It can destroy

some, whereas for others it is a crucible for the formation of godly character. Even at a time when we feel like God is silent, He is at work to develop maturity. The Lord will silence His voice at certain times in our lives, so that He can expose the condition of our hearts. There are lessons learned in stillness that cannot be learned when we are busy. There are lessons in darkness that can never be learned in the light.

In these silent times, we are able to separate our faith from our feelings. When I counsel people, I tell them not to allow their emotions to dictate their thinking. When things don't work out our way, it doesn't mean God is not with us, or we are not in His perfect will.

At times in our lives we will experience God's three answers to prayer: Yes. Not yet. No, I have something better in mind.

All of us will experience periods of loneliness and misunderstanding. Embrace them because they can bring great maturity. Press on in your prayers. Though it may seem they are just hitting the ceiling, they *are* being heard in the spiritual realm! In due time, conception and vision will become a reality. Seek the Lord. One word from God can transform your life. Hold onto it because God's Word never returns void.

So shall My word be that goes forth from My mouth; It shall not return to Me void, But it shall accomplish what I please and it shall prosper in the thing for which I sent it (Isaiah 55:11).

This is a promise of God to those who sincerely seek Him through persistent prayer in the midst of the solitary seasons in life. If it's God's word of promise, it will come to pass and prosper.

Voices of Misunderstood Women

The struggles of Hannah are not confined to a biblical character thousands of years ago. They are as relevant today as they were in Hannah's lifetime. Several months ago, a seasoned woman of faith opened up to me. She has endured many trials physically, emotionally and spiritually and always managed to keep her head up in times of despair. She gave me permission to share her testimony and insights from counseling women, who have also experienced this silent war. Here's what she wrote to me.

Voices of Today's Misunderstood Women

As misunderstood women, we slip away from our purpose, feel insignificant and become so downcast that every part of our being hurts. That is what happened to me. I found myself in a place of meaningless, nothingness and hopelessness. All of my thoughts became dark and despairing. I could not hear God because I began to pull away from Him and didn't even realize it because my sense of purpose was so clouded.

I had high hopes and big dreams but nobody knew them. I was afraid and didn't want to hurt anybody, so I didn't let anybody in. I cried alone and felt abandoned. I had a sense that I was all alone even when people were all around me, because I felt like no one really knew me.

I was always thinking about others, but felt like no one thought about me. I could not let people know I was suffering because people were depending on me. I feared that if I expressed my hurt, others might think less of me. I didn't tell people how I felt because I thought people would always remember me that way. I consoled myself with the hope that it was temporary and that it would soon go away.

I wondered how I could keep going on and what I could do to change anything. My mind wandered in many directions, searching and hoping for change. I wanted to tell others what I was going through, but no one seemed to understand. I had moments when I felt and acted like everything was okay, but then there were days of anguish and despair.

It felt like everyone else was moving forward, but I was standing still. I wasn't really envious or jealous of others; I just wanted people to know I existed and had value. My mind said there must be some good in me, so I looked for good inside and hoped it would bring me some security and pull me out of the darkness and despair.

It seemed like others talked over me, but that was partially my fault because they were not used to hearing me. Since I felt like I had nothing to contribute, I would often hold back my opinion because I believed I would be misunderstood. Even when I contributed to something, I felt shut down. I became more and more self-conscious and insecure and intentionally avoided situations that made me vulnerable or uncomfortable.

I began to question myself and everything I did, even though I tried to do everything right. I started to ask myself, "Why am I discontent when I'm trying to do everything God wants me to do?" I tried to find contentment in the simple things, but always felt empty. In this state of mind, my thoughts were like a Ping-Pong ball, back and forth, to and fro, so unstable.

I started to lose sight of myself and lost sight of my dreams, visions, passions and purpose. I was in danger of losing sight of the calling God had on my life. My body began to take on bitterness like an old, comfortable garment. In my eyes, the anger that I felt was completely justified. Even though I knew it was wrong, I became what I was fighting against.

As I began to lose myself, I wanted to find a way out. I fought to survive, knowing I had to be strong. Some people aren't strong and give in to the dread. I had to have a soldier's attitude, to say to myself, "I will fight to the end, I will keep trying everything."

When I was down at the lowest point in my life, I said to myself, "No, I will not give in. I will continue to look for a way out. I will continue to believe God and trust that He has my best interest at heart."

"I will trust that God is with me and for me and not against me. Even though no one understands me, I will hold on to the fact that God understands me. I will trust that God will make a way and give me stamina and strength and the will to love and care about others. I will not give the enemy my life. He will not win."

Someone once told me there is no one who can take your place and the purpose God created you for. What I have is what God needs. It is important to God and no one else. I held onto this. I have a special purpose. I matter and I make a difference. My God is stronger and greater and I will put my life in His hands. It's not my battle. "The battle is the Lord's."

What insights she gave to us! After reading these powerful words, I came to a deeper understanding of the emotional needs and makeup of women. We need to pray for a more discerning and sensitive ear for the people God brings into our lives. As the cliché goes, "God gave us two ears and one mouth. Perhaps we should listen more and talk less."

In my ministry, whether preaching in the streets of New York City, crusades around the world, or one-on-one witnessing, I challenge people with the two questions of life I posed earlier. "Who are you?" and "Why are you here?"

These two questions pounded in Hannah's heart. They echoed in her soul. The harder her heart pounded, the more Hannah pressed toward her miracle. She knew "who she was," a child of God. She understood "why she was here," to be used as a miracle vessel to accomplish the will of God. That is where she found the strength to go after her purpose.

I have concluded that women have two vital needs in their emotional, mental and spiritual make-up. One is love and the other is understanding. One thing that produces love and security in the heart of a wife is genuine, consistent honor and understanding from her man.

Hannah discovered that love and understanding are only truly found through an intimate relationship with God. Love is more than a feeling. To find a place of understanding requires intimate listening. Let me share ten insights into finding that place of intimate connection.

Listen without interrupting. Proverbs 18:13

Speak without accusing. James 1:19

Give without sparing. Proverbs 21:26

Pray without ceasing. Colossians 1:9

Answer without arguing. Proverbs 17:1

Share without pretending. Ephesians 4:15

Enjoy without complaint. Philippians 2:14

Trust without wavering. 1 Corinthians 13:7

Promise without forgetting. Proverbs 13:12

Forgive without punishing. Colossians 3:13

Do you feel like no one around you gets it? Do you feel like you're the only one who is misunderstood?

Jesus knows your struggle. He took your pain and nailed it to the cross. You can rest assured that you are *not* on your own. Your miracle is on the way!

CHAPTER 6

A MARRED WOMAN

And she was in bitterness of soul and prayed to the Lord *and wept in anguish* (1 Samuel 1:10).

Hannah has been marked by barrenness, bitterness and failure. Over the years, her pain has deepened and despair intensified. All of the criticism, negativity, labels and disapproval were now being internalized in Hannah's soul. Misery had set in and the decisions she was about to make would determine whether her heart would be healed or indelibly marred.

The Hebrew word for marred is shâchath. תחש A primitive root meaning: to decay, ruin, battered, cast off, corrupt, destroy or perish.[1]

The symptoms we saw in the last chapters are evidence that Hannah's heart was being marred. Her resolve was beginning to *fade*. Her dreams were in *ruins* and she was emotionally *battered*. Moreover, Hannah had an increasing sense of being *cast off* by her husband.

As difficult as life's circumstances can be, the devil's real goal is to take our struggles and magnify them. They not only inflict emotional pain and discouragement, but truly mar and disfigure the soul. Once misery sets in, bitterness is sure to follow. When the soul is marred, even the good things that come into our lives no longer bring us joy.

For Hannah, the sting of rejection, the ache of inadequacy and the disappointment of failed expectations began to penetrate every area of her life. Though she did not quit, her response in Scripture shows the damage.

First Samuel 1:10 uses these descriptive words. "She was in bitterness of soul," "wept in anguish" and "did not eat." In her narrative we see: hope marred, vision marred, dreams marred and relationships marred.

Truthfully, what *society* did to Hannah pales in comparison to seeing her husband with this evil woman. Peninnah's wickedness and envy spewed poison all over Hannah's dream. Hannah's holy desire for a happy home was subverted by Peninnah's selfishness, manipulation and sadistic provocation.

The emotional pain was intensified during days of great celebration like Passover, when everyone was filled with merriment and enjoyed the festivities. As summer turned to autumn, Elkanah and his family traveled to Shiloh to "worship and [make] sacrifice to the Lord"(1 Samuel 1:3). For Hannah, the journey was filled with strife and sadness, but for Peninnah the stage was set. It was *game time*. It was time to turn up the heat, as she took her mocking to the next level.

> *So it was, year by year, when she went up to the house of the LORD, that she provoked her; therefore she wept and did not eat* (1 Samuel 1:7).

From the hills of Ephraim in Israel, Elkanah, Hannah and Peninnah accompanied the multitudes traveling with merry hearts to Shiloh. The air was thick with joyous fervor until they reached the tabernacle. During the pilgrimages, Hannah held onto hope through every mocking assault she endured.

Deep in her heart, Hannah felt that this life was not the way God had intended it to be. She had sacrificed her happiness for her husband to produce an heir with Peninnah; but now as she looked back at the situation, she felt nothing but regret. Bitterness, anguish and sorrow saturated Hannah's heart. In order to survive, she had to mask her pain behind fake smiles and false contentment.

The Mask

In order to function in the daily responsibilities of life, people with a wounded heart carry an assortment of masks. Behind each mask is hidden pain and shame. From the very beginning, when Adam and Eve opened their soul and were seduced and contaminated by Satan, masks became the order of the day.

Let us go back to the Garden for a moment. We all know the story. We call it the *fall of man*, but what an incredible crash that was! Humanity, in self-willed disobedience, exchanged the commands of God, His perfect love and compassion, for a single bite of forbidden fruit.

We can hear the voice of God crying, "Adam, where are you?" Even though Adam did not want to face God and was hiding in shame, God came looking for him. In spite of that fact that God knows all and sees all, we find Adam and Eve hiding from Him and covering up from one another.

With their sin exposed, they had lost the covering of God's glory and saw their nakedness. Though they hid their bodies behind fig leaves, they could not cover their shame. Adam and Eve became the first in an unbroken line of humanity, whose only solution for pain was to hide from it.

Fig leaves of self-medication, excuse-making, anger and blame-shifting have become an absolute fashion necessity these days. Where these efforts have failed, people continue to hide behind materialism, codependent relationships, unbridled ambition, position, prosperity and greed.

Several years ago, when I visited Universal Studios in California, the tour guides took us on an excursion through several Hollywood sets. We saw it all and even learned the studio lingo. The *front lot* had sound stages and offices, but the *back lot* had large outdoor sets. As we viewed an amazing, intricate presentation of a city street, we stopped in front of a beautiful home. It was two stories high, with arched windows and brick siding. In my mind's eye, I pictured a door opening to a large grand staircase with a Victorian chandelier, wall hangings and furniture. To our surprise, as the tour guide flung the door open, we saw a large empty warehouse. The front wall was held up by several *2' by 4' supports*. At that moment, I realized this beautiful house was just a shell.

The tour guide went on to explain, "They call these front shells a *façade*, the French word for *false front*." Now let me ask you, "How often do you hide the marred areas of your life behind a well-dressed false front?" Perhaps your façade is your reputation, religion or regular church attendance that veils the inner emptiness of your life. Or do you hide behind your career, position or hobbies isolated in your routines, hiding the pain of a marred heart?

Think about it. What are your fig leaves or facades? Hannah's life stands as a powerful testimony to the fact that she was not delusional or in denial. She knew Peninnah's motives and had to live with them. She chose to stay quiet about her agony rather than express it until her appointed time. Even though the fig leaves of suppression could not cover up the deep marring of her soul, they seemed to be her only refuge from the enduring pain of the ongoing provocations.

Lowly Maidservant

Peninnah, high-minded and patronizing, took advantage of her motherhood to reinforce Hannah's growing belief that her unfruitful womb made her a second-class woman. Hannah no longer considered herself to be a worthy wife and saw herself as a lowly maidservant.

In her anguish, Hannah goes to the temple to seek the Lord in prayer. Three times she refers to herself as a maidservant, as she makes her plea to the Lord for a son.

Then she made a vow and said, 'O LORD of hosts, if You will indeed look on the affliction of Your <u>maidservant</u> and remember me and not forget Your <u>maidservant</u>, but will give Your <u>maidservant</u> a male child' (1 Samuel 1:11).

When Eli the high priest chastises her, in her response to him Hannah displays a lowly attitude by using the term maidservant a fourth time.

Do not consider your maidservant a wicked woman, for out of the abundance of my complaint and grief I have spoken until now (1 Samuel 1:16).

The Hebrew definition for maidservant is (אמה ' âmâh aw-maw'): Female slave–bondmaid.[2]

Although Hannah's view of herself as a maidservant is a statement of deep humility, it also reveals a lowly disposition and self-image. Marred deep inside, Hannah felt unworthy, like a female slave. Peninnah knew Hannah's condition. It was her personal mission to continuously reinforce this slave mindset.

There is no doubt that Elkanah sensed Hannah's hurt during those yearly visits to the temple. He made several attempts to show her that he loved her unconditionally. When he called his family together to partake in the holiday offering, the best portion always went to Hannah. Even this gesture did not pacify her or her broken heart.

And whenever the time came for Elkanah to make an offering, he would give portions to Peninnah his wife and to all her sons and daughters. But to Hannah he would give a double portion, for he loved Hannah (1 Samuel 1:4, 5).

Still, with a marred heart, Hannah felt further and further away from the joyous celebration each year. She could not look into Elkanah's eyes, nor find a way to truly appreciate his care and blessing. She could barely even look at her plate during the Passover meal.

Although Elkanah clearly loved her and tried his best to comfort her, like most men, he failed in his attempt to console her. He was oblivious to Peninnah's "in your face" motherhood routine, which was sheer torment for Hannah, to say the least.

Hannah's heart ached as she watched Peninnah nurse, bathe, feed and clothe each child. She was forced to accept the fact that God was using Peninnah to fill her beloved's home with the children she had always wanted.

I often wonder, was Hannah envious when she heard others say, "Oh, that

Peninnah is such a wonderful mother! Her children are beautiful."

"She can do it all."

"She makes it all seem so easy."

What about Elkanah's affirmations of Peninnah's motherhood? That kind of attention must have infected and inflamed Hannah's wounded heart. Out of her deep marring, I can hear her heart crying, "God, You created everything in this world for a reason. You have given me eyes to see, ears to hear and a mouth to speak. Why have You given me a womb, if not to bear my husband's child?"

How Long, O God?

Hannah held a deep belief in her heart that she was *meant* to be a mother. When she first married Elkanah, she dreamed of the warm home and loving family that they would create together. Now their home had become a place of heartache, loneliness and isolation for Hannah. The loving family she always dreamed, was not her own. In today's vernacular, we might say that Hannah had been "dealt a bad hand in life." I can just hear her pray as she endured the mocking, crying out to God, "How long, O God?"

I hear Hannah's cry in the life of David, the shepherd boy turned giant killer and King of Israel. He experienced seasons of loneliness and times of feeling abandoned by God. His Psalms are filled with his emotional struggles. I can see him weeping as he penned Psalm 13 that I call the "How long, O God" psalm.

How long, O LORD? Will You forget me forever? How long will You hide Your face from me? (Psalm 13:1).

How long? Have you ever said that in a prayer, feeling all alone and like God is not listening? Well, I'm right there with you! In fact, at times in my life I have felt that way with my family and visions, especially in the last six months of building our new church.

- What are the "how longs" of your life?
- How long do I have to go through this?
- How long will it take You to understand?
- How long before I get out of here?
- How long before I get a raise?
- How long before I get a better job?

- How long before I get out of debt?
- How long before I get a decent car?
- How long before we get a decent home?
- How long do I have to live like this?
- How long do I have to put up with this?

In addition to our individual "how longs," there are many feelings Hannah went through that all of us can relate to when we endure the stressful breaking points in our lives. Here are twelve statements commonly made by people under stress. Let's see if you can complete each sentence and pass the test.

1. I'm just a bundle of _____.
2. I'm at the end of my _____.
3. I'm ready to throw in the _____.
4. I'm at my wit's _____.
5. There are just not enough hours in the _____.
6. My life is falling _____.
7. I wish people would just leave me _____.
8. I feel like resigning from the human _____.
9. I haven't got any time for _____.
10. I feel like I'm running on _____.
11. I wish I was never _____.
12. I just can't take it _____.

Now, if you readily filled in the blanks, you've passed the test. You are a good candidate to become a stressed filled "how-longer." You may be asking, "Why do I have to go through these trials? Why me? Why now?"

The American Dream

As Americans, we have a certain expectation of opportunity and freedom. Our own hopes are sometimes thwarted because we have been raised with the mentality that happiness is a right.

Even America's *Declaration of Independence* begins with the famous phrase:

We hold these truths to be self-evident, that *all men are created equal,* that they are endowed by their Creator with certain unalienable rights that among these are *Life, Liberty and the pursuit of Happiness.*³

While this may be the American dream, for some the pursuit of happiness is not a reality. In some parts of the world, just to be able to eat every day and have a place to sleep is the only pursuit they know. In their struggle to merely survive, they never really get around to pursuing happiness because their life is based on persevering and surviving through great trials.

Welcome to the maturing process of life. You see, the *how longs* of life are part of the process God uses to work on us. God has an answer to our *how longs*. He says, "Until you get the revelation; until you learn the lesson. That's how long." Remember! The teacher is always silent during the test.

The Walking Dead

I have observed and experienced extreme failure first-hand. My parents fought for our country, our freedom and the opportunity to pursue the American dream. However, they both experienced the marring of their own dreams. Instead of freedom, the Jack family became imprisoned by the demons of alcohol, drugs, divorce and destroyed relationships. Some families have *Kodak* moments. Some families have *Prozac* moments. But my family had *straight jacket* moments.

Both of my parents had mental breakdowns because of our family's destructive lifestyle and the rejection they suffered. My dad's apparent steadiness and strength masked the war that raged inside of him. His strong facade began to melt away as he could no longer hide the pain. Repressed memories from being a prisoner of war in WWII began to manifest. As he struggled to hold things together, he began to break down mentally.

My middle sister Marianne, who was the peacemaker in the family, got pregnant by a young Hispanic man when she was 17. While carrying her unborn child, she was diagnosed with leukemia. Six months later, her daughter was born. Several months after the birth, consumed by cancer, Marianne died tragically. My father was completely crushed. When he came home from the funeral, he put on his robe and was overwhelmed by depression. Three weeks later, my 16-year-old sister walked into the living room and announced, "Mom, Dad, I'm pregnant!"

With everything else that had just happened, this was the final blow. Both of my parents suffered mental breakdowns and were committed to the psychiatric ward. On five separate occasions, they received electric shock treatment. My father went from a decorated hero in WWII to a 100 percent disabled veteran.

During this time no one in my family had a relationship with Jesus Christ. We only knew religion. There was no power of the Holy Spirit to hold us together. For my parents, the only logical answers were the ones that came from the psychiatrists. The doctors told them, "You need mind-controlling medication." Consequently, both mom and dad became dependent on prescription drugs.

My mom became a walking zombie. She went from a leading Civil Rights activist to a marred, meandering, deeply wounded woman. Society called her a mental case. With a cigarette hanging from her mouth, she walked in place for hours. Psychiatrists called it *marching syndrome*. She was a chain smoker and with the ulcerated wounds on her face, she looked like death warmed over. The psychotropic drugs and mental anguish broke down her immune system, which hindered the healing of the open wounds on her face.

At this point, all of my mother's dreams for her family were completely shattered. Our entire family *became* all of the negative things that society had labeled us.

As for me, being the youngest of nine, I had no curfew and did whatever I wanted to. For me, the best thing was getting high. I was caught up in the streets of Long Island and New York City, hustling to survive and keep myself sedated. I was lost and hopeless. I masked the pain with drugs and alcohol. I was on the threshold of destruction and death.

My mother eventually reached a place where she concluded that she could either accept her circumstances or *cry out to God for a miracle*. She chose to call out to God, and this decision would change the destiny of our entire family.

In His Hands

Every person is born a vessel, formed by God to fulfill the purpose He has for us. In Jeremiah 1:5, God states, "Before I formed you in the womb I knew you; before you were born I sanctified you." Throughout our lifetime, as we develop into adults, our environment, experiences, relationships and decisions all play a role in shaping us.

If you read the Bible and *hear* God's Word, you will come to realize that there are times in our lives when we are not living the way He intended for us to live. God wants us to be pure vessels filled with reverential love for Him. Think about it.

Many of us develop into people who are acceptable by worldly standards, but are out of order with God. Until we have a personal relationship with Him and understand His ways, our hearts will continue to deceive us into thinking we're "good" people. How many times have you heard someone say, "I'm a good person" and justify that claim by listing various acts of kindness?

Do you have a relationship with God?

Are you living a life that is pleasing to the Lord?

Are you fulfilling His divine purpose in your life or are you serving your own passions?

The Potter and the Clay

We are made according to God's design, yet even when we are marred by life's painful experiences He can take our lives and reshape them. As we look further into Jeremiah's prophetic word in chapter 18, God gives us a beautiful detailed video of how He can remake us. Often God *uses* difficult circumstances that *appear* to damage us, to prepare us for the fullness of our destiny.

> *Then I went down to the potter's house and there he was, making something at the wheel. And the vessel that he made of clay was marred in the hand of the potter;*
> (Jeremiah 18:3).

God told Jeremiah to think of Him as a potter. It is the potter's prerogative to decide what to do with the clay. Similarly, it is God's choice to fashion us in the way He desires. God molds us into vessels for His purpose and will. Often that process of change can be painful.

When mission teams visit our Teen Challenge center in Santiago, Dominican Republic, we take them to visit the potter's house. There is much that we can learn from the way God molds us. Understanding how a potter molds the clay is the first step in appreciating this craft.

The potter begins by pressing and stretching a piece of clay until it's free of lumps and air pockets. He then kneads and squeezes it until it becomes softer and more pliable, thus making it easier to work with.

Does this sound familiar? How many times has God stretched us and squeezed us, so He can fashion us into the vessels He desires? Sometimes we are not aware of God reshaping us. It takes the pain of being stretched to get our attention and then we're able to see that He is working to transform our lives. If the clay becomes too dry, the potter adds water to prevent it from becoming brittle and unmanageable. Trust, humility and submission moisten the clay of our character.

Once the clay is finally pliable, the potter centers the lump of clay directly in the middle of the wheel and begins to spin the shapeless mound. The potter steadies the whirling clay. This step is crucial; because if the clay is not in the correct position, it will wobble and fall over during the molding process.

Like clay, we need to be in the center of God's will. Life is not always steady and our world is often not centered. Getting to the center of God's will may be uncomfortable, but it is the most secure place to be. Our trials can wound us and leave us marred, but the Potter is always able to re-center our lives and with loving hands carefully restore and remake the vessel.

Have circumstances pushed you off center? We must submit ourselves to the hand of the Potter and allow God to keep us in the right position to be molded. It's more than good things. *God things* happen when we're at the right place, at the right time with the right heart. Submission and humility take a great deal of trust, but it is only in this place where God can complete the transformation process.

As much as we would like God to change us instantly, He is not in a hurry. God is committed to shaping our lives as we travel on this spinning wheel of life. While going through this shaping process, the water of God's Word keeps us pliable. God molds us into useful vessels. As the vessel begins to take shape, the hands of the Potter gently work the finishing touches, completing the final design.

The last step is to place the vessel into the kiln so it can be baked and made durable. It is in the kiln of the fiery trials that we encounter, that our character is solidified and matured. When the molding and shaping is done and we have gone through His purifying fire, we will be a vessel of honor, fit for His use.

And the vessel that he made of clay was marred in the hand of the potter; so he made it again into another vessel, as it seemed good to the potter to make
(Jeremiah 18:4).

Sometimes during the molding process, the vessel is damaged. God starts again taking our *marred* vessels, the *broken* chapters of our lives, and places us back on His potter's wheel. He remolds us into a useful vessel for a new chapter in our lives.

This was the molding process that God used to form Hannah into the mother of a powerful Hebrew prophet. It was His decision to close her womb for a season. She was pressed, stretched, kneaded and squeezed until she was made pliable in the Potter's hands.

The amazing thing about God's grace is that in His divine compassion, He did not discard the vessel. The marred vessel, Hannah, was now being smoothed and prepared for the center of God's will. He took the clay and made it again into another vessel, and shaped her into a woman of destiny.

Imagine the promise that this holds for us! Pastor Jim Cymbala shared, "God's grace in a Christian's life provides 10,000 new beginnings." This is the loving Potter, who created us. For those who have messed up and failed, the good news is that when we place our broken lives back into God's creative, grace-filled hands, He will *make us again*.

Naturally, we want God to supernaturally impart His character into us without any trials, but the easy road is not how God works. God desires to deal with us through *affection*; but if He can't get our attention, He'll often get it through affliction.

What appears to be marred becomes precious only with time and pressure when placed in God's hands. Through the process of life, "God transforms caterpillars into butterflies, sand into pearls and coal into diamonds."[4]

God is always faithful to answer our cry for growth. Sometimes He answers our prayers by sending a person, or putting us in a situation that will challenge us and provoke us until our flaws are revealed. Some people come into our lives as blessings and others as lessons. Through His mercy, He allows us to be tested so we may clearly see our defects and bring them to the cross.

This process purifies our hearts and builds authentic, godly character. God wants to mold us into His real deal. In order for God to prepare Hannah for her destiny, she had to learn to trust and obey through the entire molding process.

- Does it seem like your life is spinning out of control?
- Have you ever felt the pain of being marred?
- Have you been wounded by destructive relationships?
- Can you relate to Hannah's brokenness?

Has a stone-cold reality crushed your dreams of a fulfilled life, or your desire to become a success?

Even when disappointment seems to fill your life and everything around you is shaking, you can trust yourself to the Potter's hands. Like Hannah, God is preparing you for your miracle.

CHAPTER 7

INTRODUCTION TO WOMAN OF MIRACLES

From her *mission* and *marriage* to Elkanah that held such promise, we have watched Hannah's hopes deflated by the *mark* of barrenness. She was devastated as she was continuously *misunderstood*. Her soul was *marred*, attacked by a spirit of *misery* and bitterness.

Yet even through this private hell, deep inside Hannah had nurtured a measure of faith that kept hope burning in her heart. Although no one understood her pain or her vision, her hope was not dead. It was very much alive. Hannah's trials did not detour her from her vision. On the contrary, they caused her to persevere, and her hope did not disappoint her. Romans reminds us:

And not only that, but we also glory in tribulations, knowing that tribulation produces perseverance; and perseverance, character; and character, hope. Now hope does not disappoint, because the love of God has been poured out in our hearts by the Holy Spirit who was given to us (Romans 5:3-5).

Hannah held onto hope that fueled her perseverance to press on to her promise.

Let us move on to focus on the life-changing miracle process of Hannah's life. As I prepared to write this chapter, I prayed that God would help me to capture the divine progression that took place in Hannah's soul. This became the foundation for her miracle. I wondered, "What was the transitional moment in Hannah's life that took her from the precipice of despair to an exalted heroine?"

I do not claim to have the perfect prescription, a magic formula or guaranteed methodology for miracles, but I do have *God's promise*. God has the answer for every issue in life and we find it in His Word. However, we must embrace God's promise with faith and a sincere, diligent heart. The realm of God's power and promise is simply unattainable without active faith.

You cannot *seize* what you do not *see*. You must *see* your destiny by *faith*. It is *by faith* that Hannah saw God's promise. As His Word confirms:

> *Now faith is the substance of things hoped for, the <u>evidence</u> of <u>things</u> <u>not</u> <u>seen</u>*
> (Hebrews 11:1).

God will show you what He has for you if you trust Him and wait for His timing. You start this process by seeing in faith and then holding onto the vision, knowing that God will fulfill His promise. Hannah was able to see the emotional blockades to her vision and did not allow them to hinder the course of her destiny!

We have followed Hannah's journey from downcast woman, who never lost her dream, to a virtuous woman of faith. We have rejoiced in the promise of her *mission* and opened up the doors of her broken heart. We have felt her *misery* as we observed how deeply *misunderstood* she was. As we step into the miracle chapter of Hannah's life, her vision becomes reality. She persevered through four specific processes to take hold of her dream.

- Hannah examined her soul.
- Hannah went into extreme prayer.
- Hannah's strongholds were exterminated.
- Hannah expected her miracle.

EXAMINED HER SOUL

And she was in bitterness of soul and prayed to the LORD and wept in anguish. Then she made a vow and said, 'O LORD of hosts, if You will indeed look on the affliction of Your maidservant and remember me and not forget Your maidservant, but will give Your maidservant a male child, then I will give him to the LORD all the days of his life and no razor shall come upon his head.'

And it happened, as she continued praying before the LORD, that Eli watched her mouth. Now Hannah spoke in her heart; only her lips moved, but her voice was not heard. Therefore Eli thought she was drunk. So Eli said to her, 'How long will you be drunk? Put your wine away from you!'

But Hannah answered and said, 'No, my lord, I am a woman of sorrowful spirit. I have drunk neither wine nor intoxicating drink, but have poured out my soul before the LORD.' 'Do not consider your maidservant a wicked woman, for out of the abundance of my complaint and grief I have spoken until now'

(1 Samuel 1:10-16).

These seven verses define her strongholds as she assesses her condition with remarkable transparency. The accuracy of her personal inventory is amazing. At the culmination of her journey, in faith she unveils her soul with total vulnerability before God.

Her attitude is sincere. She struggles for the diagnosis; but like looking at an X-ray, she only sees the shadow of her need. Hannah needs more than X-ray insight. She needs MRI revelation.

God's MRI

The first X-ray device was discovered accidentally by the German scientist Wilhelm Röntgen in 1895. He found that a cathode-ray tube emitted invisible rays that penetrated paper and wood. The rays caused a screen of fluorescent material several yards away to glow. Roentgen used his device to examine the bone structure of a human hand. At once, it was called a "miracle" diagnostic tool. Using X-rays, Roentgen was able to make a diagnosis, even in complex cases that had previously been, at best, an informed guess.

Medical technology has advanced far beyond the X-ray, using magnetic resonance imaging called an MRI. The MRI employs the use of a magnetic field along with radio waves to create an image of the inside of the human body. It reveals much more detail and provides a deep internal view that supports a more accurate diagnosis. The MRI can scan the brain for tumors, nerve problems, bleeding and aneurysms. It can identify any organ in the body that is impaired. Because of the ability to reveal details, even bulging discs and spinal problems can all be seen by an MRI examination.[1]

As wonderful as man's technology is, there is no medical examination that can reveal the deep issues of the human soul. However, in the spiritual realm, God has something more powerful than an MRI. Through the Holy Spirit's work in Hannah's life, we can see the results of God's MRI: Miraculous Revelation Insight. God's Word serves as our spiritual MRI.

For the word of God is living and powerful and sharper than any two-edged sword, piercing even to the division of soul and spirit and of joints and marrow and is a discerner of the thoughts and intents of the heart (Hebrews 4:12).

There are 31,102 verses in the King James Bible. Every one of them is divine and God-breathed. Out of all 31,102 verses, Hebrews 4:12 defines the depth of our spiritual examination and how God's Word reveals the nature of our soul.

Hebrews 4:12 gives us insight into the illuminating power of God's Word that probes deeper than any modern technology and human understanding. Note each word: *living, powerful, piercing the soul, discerner of the thoughts and intents of the heart*. All of these words refer to spiritual examination. God's Word identifies, penetrates and magnifies the issues of the soul.

As Hannah did her spiritual inventory, the Holy Spirit revealed her strongholds, empowering her to focus on her soul. Revelation is one key to exposing and demolishing strongholds.

The Greek word for piercing is *diikneomai*. It is defined as "to go through, to penetrate or to reach through."[2] Psalm 64:6 reminds us that both the inward thoughts and the heart of man are deep. But, the depth of the heart and the magnitude of the wound are never unreachable with God's Word. It was up to Hannah to allow the Word to penetrate her soul, thus revealing and healing the wound.

A medical doctor is able to identify the epidemiology of a disease to expose the root of the sickness and to prescribe treatment by employing the perceived accuracy of an MRI. When it comes to the soul and emotions of man, God's Word reveals the sobering truth. Even with all our human understanding and wisdom, without the help of the Holy Spirit and the Word of God (God's

MRI), our minds cannot discern the intents of *our very own hearts*.

The heart is deceitful above all things and desperately wicked; <u>who can know it?</u> I, the LORD, search the heart; I test the mind, even to give every man according to his ways, according to the fruit of his doings (Jeremiah 17:9-10).

God searches the heart and reveals the condition of the soul. For example, King David was a man after God's own heart. Still, he knew that even with all of his victories as a shepherd, giant killer, psalmist and warrior king, only God could expose the underlying motives, wickedness and selfish intent of his own heart.

We experience true security only when we allow God to search our hearts. We find peace only when we walk in integrity, honesty and complete transparency before God. I've learned that, "Nothing will attract God's favor upon your life like a transparent heart that refuses to pretend."

Consider King David's soul-searching cry in the writing of his Psalms:

Examine me, O LORD and prove me; try my mind and my heart

(Psalm 26:2, 3).

Search me, O God and know my heart; try me and know my anxieties; And see if there is any wicked way in me and lead me in the way everlasting

(Psalm 139:23, 24).

I believe that Hannah recognized her soul was infected. She was in danger of being paralyzed by the cancer of discouragement and the bitterness that tried to poison her vision. We can see the deep, emotional expression of Hannah's pain when she poured out her heart to the Lord. As she prayed, God brought not only her wounds, but her strongholds, to the surface where they could be dealt with.

Hannah placed herself in the examination room of divine truth when she went to the temple. Her understanding of truth was not based on feeling, emotion or social status. In Hannah's oppressed condition, she could not trust her wounded emotions. She did not rely on what she felt, but held onto what God had planted in her heart. She did not allow her emotions to dictate her actions or define her destiny. Her plumbline was God's design and divine plan for her life according to His Word.

Are You A "DJ?"

In over 25 years of ministry, I've encountered both men and women with explosive manifestations of bitterness and anger that arose from carrying an illegal cargo deep within their soul. They often searched for answers within themselves and others as to why they lost control and exploded. I would encourage them to look past the surface, beyond the outburst, to find the root of the pain. Rather than wasting time blame-shifting and pointing fingers, with God's sharp Word, I would help them cut through their artificial shield of protection. I call this shield, "DJ," an acronym for "defend and justify."

When people DJ, or *defend* and *justify* their deadly defects, they dance in denial around the real issues of life. They empower their strongholds, and denial becomes the enabling "dance partner."

The dance masks the real problem and the deadly reality of the issues that are the controlling force of their emotions. Escape becomes a co-dependent partner that helps them to cope with the rough times, rather than experience legitimate victory by embracing the truth and experiencing the power of God. These instinctive survival mechanisms are the symptoms of deep denial. This is the profile of a person living with a wounded, bitter heart.

Proverbs 16:25 says, "There is a way that seems right to a man, but its end is the way of death." This verse describes the end of a blind, bitter DJ's journey to a "T."

It is interesting to note the noun *way* and adjective *right* in Proverbs 16. When you confuse the ways that seem right, the result can be deadly. For example, in Hebrew, the word *right* means "convenient, well-pleased," and the word *way* means "a habitual course of life."

Wounded, bitter people tend to live their lives in denial. They develop survival mechanisms that defend and justify their "ways" thus protecting their infected soul because it feels "right." The greatest danger of living in denial is believing that this attitude is the *proper* response to a "convenient, well-pleasing, habitual course of life." Wounded people often interpret the "way" of life through their feelings that seem "right." God's Word makes it very clear that this frame of mind is the "way of death."

People in denial tend to also have the following thought process: "I must defend myself, my world and my territory. It feels right, it keeps me alive and I will survive. I am okay. That's just how it is and how I need to deal with it." What they do not realize is that they are destroying their relationships, detouring their future and ultimately derailing their destiny.

Denial can run so deep that these responses are justified as *normal* reactions. They become such a part of everyday life that, though they hurt everyone around them, they tend to wonder what is wrong with *everyone else*. Angry eruptions become a defense mechanism to control conflict or correction and protect a bitter soul. I've come to realize that *the ones that hurt others the most, have been hurt the deepest*. As is often said, "Hurt people, hurt people."

These defense mechanisms slam the door on the people God sends to help them. They forfeit any chance of being vulnerable enough to see the truth and to receive healing. As a consequence, patience, willingness to help and trust are sacrificed. Relationships are damaged. Marriages are eroded and become stale. Intimacy dies. A once loving, romantic relationship becomes numb and robotic. Loyal, loving robes become betrayal rags.

Hannah on the other hand refused to walk in denial. With every affliction Hannah endured, she never took the easy way out. She intently examined herself and identified each stronghold that gripped her soul. Look with me as Hannah's inward struggles are exposed in 1 Samuel 1. She was willing to...

- **ADMIT**: In verse 10, she *admits* that she is in "bitterness of soul" and "anguish."
- **ASK:** In verse 11, she *asks* God to "indeed look on the affliction of your maidservant."
- **CONFESS:** In verse 15, she *confesses* a "sorrowful spirit."
- **RELEASE:** In verse 16, she releases her "abundance of complaint and grief."

As God's MRI gave fresh revelation, Hannah was able to see the cancerous tumors in her soul. This examination brought her to a place where repentance prepared her for healing and deliverance. She declared in her prayer that deadly strongholds were not going to stop her.

Mom's Unforgettable Day

Like Hannah, deep in her heart my mother was hungry for God. She joined many churches that offered traditional Christian religion, but our family needed more than religion. My mother needed the One who could heal her sickness and change her family. We needed a personal encounter with the One who created it all.

Alone in her bedroom one night, my mother stared blankly at the dim glow of a tiny 13-inch black-and-white TV. Even with a piece of aluminum foil wrapped around the tip of the antenna, she could not find a clear signal. Her hands trembled, turning the tuner to find a channel, as she fought the relentless roar to surrender to despair.

Wanting God to take her life, she was ready to die. Desperate to escape the misery she had endured for years, she collapsed on her bed. Suddenly, she heard a message of hope coming from the television. As her sick body turned over to watch and listen, the voice sounded familiar. It was Billy Graham preaching a message of hope and healing from a televised crusade.

He spoke of a healing Jesus, a personal Jesus who was "Wounded for our transgressions, bruised for our iniquities...and by His stripes we are healed" (Isaiah 53:5). These words penetrated her heart and distraught mind. He pointed her to Jesus, the One who could not only heal her, but set her and her whole family free.

In that instant, deep within the recesses of my mother's broken heart, there was a glimmer of hope. Billy Graham gave an invitation to receive Jesus as personal Lord and Savior. She knew that the only chance she had was to act on this truth immediately.

As she wobbled down the stairs and burst out of the front door of our house, with her ulcerated face, scabby lips and matted hair, she knelt at the curb and cried out to God. With her hands raised to the heavens, she pleaded, "Help me, God! Save me. Save my family!" God's Word, His MRI, penetrated my mother's heart and the journey to her miracle redemption began.

Hannah was on a journey for her miracle as well. She examined her soul, saw the bitterness built up in her heart and knew the bitterness had to be removed for God to answer her prayer. Recognizing that these strongholds were alive and deadly, she forged ahead. She brought everything to the altar and poured out her soul to the Lord, trusting God to destroy the strongholds and resurrect her dream.

If Hannah met with such success under the covenant of law and death, imagine how much more freedom is available to us through the covenant of life. God's Word gives us revelation of truth, healing and freedom. The Bible is filled with over 2,500 promises that will set any captive free.

Then Jesus said to those Jews who believed Him, 'If you abide in My word, you are My disciples indeed. And you shall know the truth and the truth shall make you free' (John 8:31, 32).

Jesus answered them, 'Most assuredly, I say to you, whoever commits sin is a slave of sin. And a slave does not abide in the house forever, but a son abides forever. Therefore if the Son makes you free, you shall be free indeed' (John 8:34-36).

Hannah searched her heart, examined her soul, uncovered her strongholds and prepared herself to press into God's presence through extreme prayer determined to go after her miracle.

EXTREME PRAYER

And it happened, as she continued praying before the LORD, that Eli watched her mouth. Now Hannah spoke in her heart; only her lips moved, but her voice was not heard (1 Samuel 1:12, 13).

Deep in her heart, Hannah knew that the antidote to her misery, the open door to her miracle, was to be in the supernatural presence of God's throne room and to pour out her soul to the Lord. Prayer is the heartbeat of every child of God. Every great mission, deliverance, healing and victory, every miracle intervention and provision is birthed in prayer.

Communion With God

Most of us know the basics of prayer. We have been taught on the *need* to pray, preached to on *how* to pray and *heard* our mothers, fathers, grandparents or pastors pray. The *type* of prayer that Hannah entered into is called "travail." Simply defined, travail is *when a prayer becomes a cry*.

Travail touches the heart of God and carries you into the heavenly realm. If you examine the great victories of the patriarchs, you will see how their *prayers became cries*. King David is called the weeping psalmist. Jeremiah is known as the weeping prophet. Whether it was Moses, Abraham, Isaac, or Jacob, Paul or Peter in the New Testament or powerful women of faith like Rahab, Deborah, Ruth, Esther or Mary, their *prayers* became *cries* as they called out to God.

Rahab in Joshua 2:1-7

Deborah in Judges 4:4

Ruth in the Book of Ruth

Esther in the Book of Esther

Mary in Luke 1

Surrendering To God

The greatest example of travail is Jesus in the Garden of Gethsemane. It is here, through Jesus' example of a surrendered soul of supplication, that God's redemptive oil was produced. Remember, *Gethsemane* means the *olive press*. How appropriate that this place of travail was named Gethsemane; we can all identify with life's olive press.

The biblical word that clearly expresses travail is *supplication*. Supplication is a prayer of total surrender of your will to God's will. Hebrews 5 describes "supplication" in the life of Jesus.

> *Who, in the days of His flesh, when He had offered up <u>prayers</u> and <u>supplications</u>, with <u>vehement cries</u> and <u>tears</u> to Him who was able to save Him from death and was heard because of His godly fear, though He was a Son, yet He learned obedience by the things which He <u>suffered</u>* (Hebrews 5:7, 8).

This passage of Scripture details Jesus' Gethsemane experience where His prayer transcended into surrendered supplication. With vehement cries, in loving obedience, He embraced God's will to go to the cross. The word *vehement* means an inner passionate, fervent, vigorous cry. Although this cry is emotionally painful, it ushers you into the presence and securing peace of God.

The promise of Philippians 4 reminds us that prayer and supplication are not only a mandate, but a pathway to God's power and gateway to God's presence.

> *Be anxious for nothing, but in everything by <u>prayer</u> and <u>supplication</u>, with thanksgiving, let your <u>requests</u> be made known to God; and the peace of God, which surpasses all understanding, will guard your hearts and minds through Christ Jesus*
> (Philippians 4:6, 7).

For us, supplication is the wit's end of prayer when there are no more options.

Allow me to share a teaching on supplication by one of my mentors, David Wilkerson. I'm so thankful for his example of Christ and the personal times I had with him as he poured into my life with lessons on prayer. Brother Dave, as his sons in the Lord called him, was a holy man known for his prayer. He lived his life in travail and supplication. In one of his devotions, he defines supplication as follows:

> *"The word supplication is never used in the Bible except to denote a cry or prayer. The Hebrew word for supplication signifies 'an olive branch wrapped with lamb's wool, or some kind of cloth, waved by a supplicant seeking peace or surrender.' These were called branches of supplication. Simply put, they were flags that signified a cry of total, unconditional surrender.*

> *"Picture a battle-weary soldier, ragged and worn, tired and overwhelmed, stuck in a foxhole of self-will. He is all alone, weary and haggard and has come to the end of himself. He breaks a branch off a tree and ties his white undershirt to it,*

lifts it and crawls out of his foxhole, crying, 'I surrender. I give up!'

"That is supplication! It says, 'I surrender! I can't fight this battle anymore, I'm lost and despairing.'

"Supplication is not just calling on God to do what you want. It is not begging and pleading with Him to assist you in your plans. On the contrary, it is a total giving up of your will and your way!"

Supplication, however, has a more victorious ending than the soldier giving up. Convinced that he is surrendering to the enemy, the battle-weary soldier emerges from the fox hole expecting to be captured by the enemy. Suddenly, he has a glorious revelation that he is being rescued by his own military force! This is a picture of a victorious ending that becomes a new beginning as the result of supplication to God.

Crying Out To God

As Hannah travailed in supplication in the temple, she began to understand that God was bringing her to a place of total submission. This was her olive branch and lamb's wool sign of surrender. As she responded to Eli's accusation of being drunk, she said, "I poured out my soul to the Lord." In that moment, the curtain of revelation opened.

Hannah was able to see what God had prepared for her all along. It was as though Jesus was standing there, pulling back the veil so she could see the miraculous answer to her prayer. She would have never been able to see behind that curtain to the revelation, until she surrendered every fiber of her being to the Lord. *Travail is not God partnering with us, but us surrendering to God.*

Through deep travail, Hannah's pain, misery and barrenness were transformed into the "oil of prayer." This process of supplication yields the oil of faith, the oil of forgiveness, the oil of freedom and the oil of favor. If you truly desire to have a stronghold broken in your life and experience the favor of God, you will have to experience the *olive press* of prayer.

In my upcoming book *Fuel for Your Fire*, I share about "The Gethsemane Experience" detailing Jesus' emotional, mental and spiritual encounter in the transitional hours that prepared Him for the cross. In His hour of isolation, Jesus went into prayer and asked His disciples to watch with Him and pray. When Jesus needed them the most, they fell short by falling asleep.

There are seasons when you feel all alone, misunderstood and have no one to trust or share your feelings with. It is at that critical time that you must press on. God will always meet you there. Do you find yourself in a place of nothingness? I recently read this description of that place.

There is a time and place in our walk with God in which He sets us in a place of isolation and waiting. It is a place in which all past experiences are of no value.

It is a time of such stillness that it can disturb the most faithful if we do not understand that He is the one who has brought us to this place for only a season. It is as if God has placed a wall around us. No new opportunities-simply inactivity.

During these times, God is calling us aside to fashion something new in us. It is a place of nothingness designed to call us to deeper roots of prayer and faith. It is not a comfortable place, especially for a task-driven workplace believer. Our nature cries out, "You must do something" while God is saying, "Be still and know that I am God" (Psalm 46:10).

You know the signs that you have been brought into this place when He has removed many things from your life and you can't seem to change anything. Perhaps you are unemployed. Perhaps you are laid up with an illness.

Many people live a very planned and orchestrated life where they know almost everything that will happen. But for people in whom God is performing a deeper work, He brings them into a time of quietness that seems almost eerie. They cannot see what God is doing. They just know that He is doing a work that cannot be explained to themselves or to others.

Has God brought you to a place of nothingness? Be still and know that He really is God. When this happens, your nothingness will be turned into something you will value for the rest of your life.[1]

He Prayed More Earnestly

Luke's Gospel holds the key to Jesus' victory in this trial in Gethsemane.

And being in agony, He prayed more earnestly. Then His sweat became like great drops of blood falling down to the ground (Luke 22:44).

Note the progression of Jesus' prayer when Luke specifically points out, *"He prayed more earnestly."* Earnestly means intently. When trials get harder, when burdens get heavier and temptations become more intense, a child of God must follow the example of the Master and pray more earnestly. Jesus travailed so deeply that *His sweat became like great drops of blood.*

Travail causes an eruption in the soul. Your mind, will and emotions connect with God's Spirit in prayer in such a deep intensity that it loosens the roots of strongholds. Jesus' travail and supplication were so intense that the capillaries in His forehead exploded and blood seeped from the pores of His brow. This type of prayer penetrates hell, reaches the heavens and moves God's hand.

As you are reading this chapter, you may be experiencing a mighty trial in your life and thinking, "I don't know what to pray, or even how to pray through this torment." A profound example of extreme prayer (travail) is found in the Book of Romans.

Likewise the Spirit also helps in our weaknesses. For we do not know what we should pray for as we ought, but the Spirit Himself makes intercession for us with groanings which cannot be uttered (Romans 8:26).

God's Word promises us that when we don't know how to pray, we can cry out in surrendered supplication, and the Holy Spirit will pray in us, through us and for us.

There will be times in your life when things are so messed up that you can't even find the right words to pray. Your vocabulary is depleted; you say, "God, I don't know what to say. My prayer words are all used up and I still feel empty. I don't know how to pray, but help my son, help my daughter, help my baby, help my marriage, help my family, help *me*, O God!"

When you don't know how to pray, the Bible says the Holy Spirit makes intercession for you with groanings that cannot be uttered. The prayer comes from deep within your soul as you begin to groan and weep. Travail is when tears are pouring down and you have no words to express. The cry flows from the depth of your soul.

Do you remember the woman who washed Jesus' feet with her tears and dried them with her hair? (Luke 7:37, 38). Did you ever wonder how she did that?

Psalm 56:8 says, "You number my wanderings; Put my tears into Your bottle."

These precious women took this Scripture literally. Some had tear cloths or napkins. Many Hebrew women who were familiar with this Psalm had their own personal tear bottles. When they experienced pain, frustration, rejection and hurt in their lives, as they wept they held the tear bottle to their eyes. They collected their teardrops to preserve them. The tear bottle was a memorial unto God that He heard their cries and would answer their deepest prayers. I can see Mary coming to Jesus pouring out her tears over the Son of God as a loving memorial.

Tears in Scripture play a unique role in spiritual breakthrough. They are like seeds sown in brokenness that will not only bring forth a spiritual harvest of results, but also rejoicing. Charles H. Spurgeon refers to travail as a "ministry of tears" and "liquid prayer."

- There are many types of tear prayers.
- There are tears of sorrow or suffering.
- There are tears of joy.
- There are tears of compassion.
- There are tears of desperation.
- There are tears of travail or giving birth.
- There are tears of repentance.

"Don't ever discount the wonder of your tears. They can be healing waters and a stream of joy. Sometimes they are the best words the heart can speak."[2]

As she poured her liquid treasure, she was saying, "Jesus, thank You for being there for me. Now I want to give my tears back to You. I want to anoint Your feet." When you come to that place, where your prayer becomes a cry, the power of God moves demonic forces, releases God's promise and glorious miracles happen.

The Power of Prayer

Jesus also demonstrated prayer that becomes a cry at the death of His dear friend Lazarus. As Jesus was coming to speak life back into his friend's soul and call him from the tomb, the Scriptures address two clear dynamics: *His love for his friend* and *His travail of intercession.*

- *First,* consider Jesus' love for his friend. "Therefore the sisters sent to Him, saying, 'Lord, behold, he whom You love is sick'" (John 11:3).

  It is wonderful to know that Jesus loved Lazarus so deeply and how much He loves you and me. Not only is He our Savior, but a devoted, loving Friend. He feels our pain and comforts us in our sorrow.

- *Second,* Jesus groans in deep travail for his friend. "Therefore, when Jesus saw her weeping and the Jews who came with her weeping, He groaned in the spirit and was troubled" (John 11:33).

Note what happens as Jesus approached the tomb of Lazarus. Lazarus had been dead for four days. "Then Jesus, again *groaning* in Himself, came to the tomb" (John 11:38). This groaning was a prelude to the miracle that was about to happen.

Then they took away the stone from the place where the dead man was lying. And Jesus lifted up His eyes and said, 'Father, I thank You that You have heard Me. And I know that You always hear Me, but because of the people who are standing by I said this, that they may believe that You sent Me.' Now when He had said these things, He cried with a loud voice, 'Lazarus, come forth!' (John 11:41-43).

The miracle came as the resurrection power of heaven was ignited by extreme prayer.

And he who had died came out bound hand and foot with grave clothes and his face was wrapped with a cloth. Jesus said to them, 'Loose him and let him go'

(John 11:44).

Before Lazarus could walk in the newness of life, Jesus had to instruct His disciples to get the grave clothes off of him. This same power was stirring in Hannah's soul. She was on the verge of having this resurrection power released within her.

We all have our own grave clothes of unforgiveness, negative thinking, lack of self-worth and self-centeredness. These grave clothes don't produce life. They lead to death.

Jesus is *still saying* today, "Loose him and let him go." This Scripture is a word addressed to all that are bound by affliction and the wounds of emotional abuse. Although you may be able to function, the grave clothes of misery, betrayal, hurt and bitterness must be removed before you can be loosed and set free.

The grave clothes on Hannah's life were now being revealed. As Hannah poured out her soul to the Lord in extreme prayer, in groanings that could not be uttered, her travail was preparing her soul to exterminate every stronghold that blocked her miracle.

In bitterness of soul, Hannah wept in anguish. It was a painful implosion of the heart. It was a dynamic of travail that expressed the bewailing pain of the soul experienced at the death of a loved one. Hannah was at the threshold of *emotional* death, bringing her soul to the Lord.

Relief and Hope

Here in Long Island, women of all ages, with battered and broken hearts, come to our beautiful Teen Challenge restoration homes. Their lives have been devastated by abusive relationships, abortions, incest, rape, prostitution and alcohol and drug addiction. These women come from New York, New Jersey and other parts of the country seeking healing, hope and a future. Like Hannah, who poured out her soul in prayer, these precious ladies pour out their souls in travail.

On Wednesday nights, our congregation and Teen Challenge students, staff and their families gather at Freedom Chapel for a night of prayer and worship. As I lead these powerful prayer services, I hear the cries of travail and supplication that pour out from wounded souls.

Some of the greatest breakthroughs take place as women (and men) seek God during the prayer service and allow the Word of God to do its work. I always emphasize to our congregation that Wednesday night prayer service is our most important service of the week.

As Jesus declared, "My House shall be called a house of prayer" (Matthew 21:13). These prayer services become a birthing chamber of miracles. My heart rejoices as I see our people enter God's presence and go beyond the curtain to their miracle.

In extreme prayer, we surrender our entire being to Almighty God and invite Him to intervene in our lives. Like Hannah, as we pour out our hearts, God will meet us at our point of need. As we totally surrender to the Lord, He moves in a way that will never happen otherwise.

E.M. Bounds challenges us, *"How vast are the possibilities of prayer! It lays its hand on God Almighty and moves Him to do what He would not otherwise do if prayers were not offered."* Hannah's extreme prayer released the power of God and loosed the roots of the strongholds that infiltrated her heart.

Praying at the Threshold

After praying with Billy Graham, my mother had her own experience of extreme prayer as she knelt down in the street crying out to God. It was here that my mother spiritually lifted up the olive branch with the lamb's wool in supplication. She had travailed in her bedroom as her prayer became a cry that broke through the heavenlies. Her prayer resounded in the inner chambers of the throne room of heaven.

At the time I was 15 years old, and hanging out at the end of the block. One of my friends came running up to me shouting, "Your mom's gone crazy again! She's kneeling on the street, praying and crying out to God!"

I immediately ran down the street yelling, "Stop, Mom! Stop it right now! Get back in the house. Don't you ever embarrass me like this again!"

I was angry. I thought we were going to have to take her back to the hospital again. However, looking back, I realize that all of our miracles *began* when my mother's knees hit the pavement, crying out to heaven in deep travail. Like Hannah, my mother's prayers transcended human words that expressed her inner pain.

In the *supernatural*, God's hand was ready to loosen every chain that bound my mother and release her from the personal prison where she had suffered for years. God tore off her grave clothes as she was now on the threshold of a generational miracle.

Throughout the Bible, Jesus is described *sitting* at the right hand of God the Father. However, in your time of desperate need, Jesus *stands* in intercession for you. God's Word gives us a glimpse of what Jesus does when His son or daughter cries out in affliction.

In the New Testament, Stephen was a great man of faith. In Acts 7, he was being stoned for his faith in Jesus. With his last breath, this martyr gives us a glimpse of *his vision of Jesus* in heaven.

> *When they heard these things they were cut to the heart and they gnashed at him with their teeth. But he, being full of the Holy Spirit, gazed into heaven and saw the glory of God, and <u>Jesus standing at the right hand of God</u> and said, 'Look! I see the heavens opened and the <u>Son of Man standing at the right hand of God</u>!'*
>
> (Acts 7:54-56).

Since the Word of God declares that Jesus Christ is *seated* at the right hand of the Father, the Holy Spirit's revelation to Stephen in that moment was extremely significant. He saw Jesus was not sitting, but standing. He is ever interceding for us, especially in the most desperate moments of our lives.

Never forget, that in that moment of pain as you carry burdens beyond your ability to endure, you can cry out in travail and supplication. As you do,

Jesus is not sitting, but standing with you in divine intercession.

It was at this place of extreme prayer that Hannah encountered the power of faith at a new level. Extreme prayer prepared her heart and ignited Hannah's faith to exterminate the strongholds in her life.

EXTERMINATE THE STRONGHOLDS

But Hannah answered and said, 'No, my lord, I am a woman of sorrowful spirit. I have drunk neither wine nor intoxicating drink, but have poured out my soul before the LORD' (1 Samuel 1:15).

Strongholds gripped Hannah's soul and threatened to block the birth of her vision. In order to receive her miracle, Hannah had to prepare her heart and position herself for God to pull down those strongholds.

In the physical realm, a stronghold is a fortified place; a guarded territory, a place of security or survival or a place dominated by a particular group. Strongholds are structures, often castles or fortresses, built on an elevated land mass, geographically positioned to strategically defend against enemy attack.

In Hebrew, the word for stronghold is:

בָּגְשָׂב miśgâb; (mis-gawb') - a lofty or inaccessible place; a refuge; defense, high fort, a tower.[1]

In the spiritual realm, a stronghold is a fortress built around emotional wounds to protect injured territory.

Stronghold is not a word used in everyday conversation. It is a compound word containing two common words, *strong* and *hold*. It denotes a forceful grip that locks you in and keeps you where you are.

Castles and Fortresses

As a speaker in conferences throughout Great Britain, I had the opportunity to explore the castles that adorn the beautiful Welsh, English and Scottish countryside. One of my favorites was Stirling Castle, one of the largest and most important castles in Scotland, both historically and architecturally. It sits atop Castle Hill, which forms part of the Stirling Sill geological formation.

Surrounded on three sides by steep cliffs, Stirling Castle has an almost invincible, defensive position. Many adversaries attempted to attack, but its location on top of the mountain, coupled with its tall, thick walls, kept those who lived inside secure from attack. Over the years, enemies who tried to conquer the fortress consistently failed.

Looking back, I'm reminded of 2 Corinthians 10:4, "For the weapons of our warfare *are* not carnal but mighty in God for pulling down strongholds."

In his book, *Sparkling Gems From the Greek*, author Rick Renner defines the ancient meaning of a stronghold.

> *The word 'stronghold' comes from the ancient Greek word ochuroma. It is one of the oldest words in the New Testament, originally used to describe a fortress.*
>
> *It depicted a fortress, a castle, or a citadel. By 57 A.D., when Paul wrote Corinthians, the word ochuroma was also used to describe a prison. Since most secure, highly guarded prisons were usually constructed deep inside such fortresses, it makes sense that the word for a fortress or stronghold is the identical Greek word for a prison.*[2]

You might ask, what is the difference between a *stronghold* and a *prison*? A *stronghold* is built for protection to keep others *out*, whereas a *prison* is built to keep someone *in*. The natural consequence of both is that the walls keep us from experiencing real freedom.

The strongholds Hannah fought were a destructive force that towered over her and kept her in an emotional prison. When Hannah stated, "I've held my complaint until now," she was telling Eli that she wasn't letting anyone in and she wasn't letting anything out – until now.

When I minister to wounded people, I meet some who are locked up in their own personal *prison* and others in so much pain that they have constructed impenetrable *strongholds* to protect their wounds. Untreated, these wounds will hold them in a *life sentence*, or should I say, *death sentence* of bitterness. Strongholds in the soul hinder emotional stability and impede spiritual growth.

Spiritually speaking, the "strongholds" the Bible refers to are lies that I call the "satanic frequencies of hell." Deception enters through the gateway of our mind, through insecure emotions that arise from unfilled expectations, failures, painful experiences and the wounds of abuse and betrayal.

In our minds, strongholds are built in the "high place" of our thoughts and emotions. Even when logic tells us that the enemy's words are untrue, open painful wounds still continue to receive and reproduce the lies that wage war in our souls. They alter our perspective of truth. They sabotage all sense of self-worth and self-image.

Deeply ingrained in our minds and belief systems, strongholds twist our emotions. When we give them power, they can exert full control over our lives.

When a *lie* becomes your reality, the *reality* that you believe has consequences. Your perspective, discernment, decision making and responses become distorted. You end up blocking, resisting and rejecting wise counsel and continue to live in a mental and emotional prison. When slapped in the face with a reality check, also known as the truth, you become bitter because you can't handle the truth.

Victim Turned Villain

Many people who carry bitterness have a distorted perspective. They try to function while still holding onto the offenses of people who wounded them. This attitude produces a *victim* mentality. They convince themselves that unless the circumstances or people around them change, their wounds will never heal.

When we hold on to wounding experiences, we give the wounds and offenders power over our lives that continues long after the offense, betrayal or trauma have ended. While a person may have been truly violated and victimized, the question is, "What do I do next?"

We all have been hurt in one way or another, some deeper than others. But, if we don't let go of the violation and forgive the violator, we the victim can become the violator. When victims hold onto the violation, it becomes the driving force of their life. Those abused become the abusers. The victims turn into a villain. The villains then become vigilantes seeking vengeance to relieve their pain.

As the vigilantes' heart becomes even more bitter, they believe that vengeance and vindication will bring them healing and freedom. The victim-turned-villain becomes the enemy of their very own soul, sabotaging relationships, setting off torpedoes that ignite the hidden explosives in their wounded soul.

An ancient Chinese proverb says, *"If you're in pursuit of vengeance, be sure to dig two graves."*[3]

St. Augustine, a great Christian thinker said, *"If you are suffering from a bad man's injustice, forgive him lest there be two bad men."*[4]

Hannah endured *repeated* attacks from Peninnah that could have inflamed her wounds and clouded her perspective. However, her determination to hold onto her dream gave her hope.

Even though people may have seen her as a victim (which she was), her resolve to press forward prevented her from becoming a villain. Hannah knew deep down inside, even amidst the strongholds that gripped her soul, she could not let a victim mentality distort her faith and steal her dream. She never retaliated for the abuse she endured.

When there is a stronghold in your mind or in your emotions, you may not see the roughhewn *stones* of bitterness, misery, anguish and sorrow. These *stones* become the building blocks that create invisible walls that act as *both* fortress and prison. Like the walls of a castle, they isolate you from anyone trying to *break in* to help you to see the truth that will *break you out* and set you free.

Over the years, while counseling deeply wounded individuals, one of the greatest challenges is to help them tear down the indiscernible barriers that surround their mind and emotions. If the power of God does not demolish the bondage that Satan has enforced on their minds, that are at the root of their addiction, they will remain captive. Imprisoned by the lies, they turn hope into discouragement, security into worry and faith into doubt. Victory only comes when they get the revelation that they can be set free by the power and blood of Jesus Christ and the truth of His Word.

I was recently contacted by a woman named Tammy. She was in her mid-40s when she graduated Teen Challenge. She went on to serve in our ministry and was an effective outreach worker and leader. About two years after her graduation, while faithfully serving with us, she became emotionally involved with an unstable man.

As executive director of Teen Challenge and her pastor, I lovingly confronted her and cautioned her about the dangers of this unhealthy relationship. I ministered a godly warning and shared the consequences of moving forward in this relationship.

Tammy refused the godly counsel and rebelled, left the ministry and married this man. Her relationship quickly soured, leading to a very painful divorce. Over the next ten years, every time I saw her, her greeting to me was abrupt and withdrawn.

Holding onto the offense, she turned it into a stronghold of bitterness. She had resisted a loving warning from God that would have protected her from years of pain. Paralyzed by unforgiveness, she had been held captive in her own stronghold of offense for years. Because of her distorted perception of truth, she had sentenced *herself* to a ten-year prison term of bitterness and hardness of heart.

While I was writing this chapter, she called me one night broken and very repentant. She tearfully confided, "Pastor Jimmy, I need to ask you for forgiveness. I've been holding on to resentment against you. I spent many years fighting against a wall which turned out to be myself. Holding onto painful memories and offenses made me a very angry and bitter person. I had to take ownership for the decisions I made in my life. I'm not happy about the time I've wasted in rebellion and foolishness, but I'm very glad that God is truly the redeemer He says He is!

"The scales have fallen from my eyes. I am *now* able to take full responsibility for my past decisions and their consequences."

Tammy's sincere apology and admission of a self-inflicted wound blessed my heart. By the time the conversation was over, Tammy and I rejoiced in her freedom and fresh perspective on life. She recently told me, "I can't believe how blind I was and how I blamed everybody for my foolish, fleshly mistake. I am so free today and *now* have a secure joy in my life with Jesus and all my relationships."

Friends, remember this: It is God's purpose to *uncover the lie*, so we can *discover the truth* and *recover the promise* of all that God has called us to be.

The strongholds in Hannah's soul were determined to keep her bound in an *inner prison* that she could not break out of on her own. As defined in 2 Corinthians 10:4-5, strongholds can be broken only by the authority of God's Word. When the apostle Paul continues "casting down arguments and every high thing that exalts itself against the knowledge of God, bringing every thought into captivity to the obedience of Christ," he is speaking directly to the fortresses and prisons that captivate our minds.

Unattended, our minds become the devil's workshop, where he crafts thoughts, memories and mental videos of the offenses that torment us. His workshop needs to be shut down, gutted out and a final eviction notice delivered to the devil.

Like Hannah and every person who has been freed from the prisons of abuse, misery, bitterness and unforgiveness, you must bring "every thought captive to the obedience of Christ" (2 Corinthians 10:5).

Can you see any strongholds in your life?

- Do you feel like a hostage of any of these areas in your mind, will and emotions?
- Are there areas of your mind that are currently controlled by the enemy's lies of fear, doubt or worry?
- Are you tormented by past wounds and unforgiveness?

- Do you find yourself being repeatedly attacked in the areas of your self-worth and self-image?
- Are these attacks debilitating and crippling you?
- Do you feel imprisoned, paralyzed and unable to fully express who you really are?

If you answered *yes* to any of these questions, you may have allowed offenses or wounds to become deadly strongholds in your life. These strongholds alter your mental and emotional perception and hinder you from stepping out to experience the abundant life that God has promised you.

Hide and Seek

One problem is that people allow strongholds to hook themselves into their souls. They hide behind their walls instead of letting God root them out. The origin of the great "hide and seek" can be traced back to the very beginning.

After Eve disobeyed God and invited Adam to join her, they covered themselves with fig leaves in a vain attempt to hide their shame and insecurity. Then, when they heard God calling for them, they hid from Him in the garden.

And they heard the sound of the Lord God walking in the garden in the cool of the day, and Adam and his wife hid themselves from the presence of the Lord God among the trees of the garden (Genesis 3:8).

Can you picture Adam and Eve hiding behind the trees, convinced that God would not find them there? I can only conclude that disobedience dulls your intelligence. Let's face it, sin makes you stupid! This was the first hide-and-seek game in human history and they got caught!

I am so glad that Hannah refused to play *hide and seek*. She removed the fig leaves in order to present herself transparent before God. No more fronting, facades, or false smiles. She let it all out.

Mankind has never found a fig leaf that can cover sin and the insecurity that it brings. To this day, people still look for fig leaves, superficial solutions like self-esteem, money and even religious works. All external acts of religion, apart from the eternal atoning sacrifice of Jesus Christ on Calvary, are withered fig leaves in the face of His unspeakable gift of mercy, grace, forgiveness and love.

Remember, God can only *cover* what we *uncover*. Until we come to a place of transparency and vulnerability that allows us to open up to God, His love and mercy is unable to cover us.

God asked Adam and Eve, "Who told you that you were naked?" Adam and Eve's nakedness, prior to Satan's seduction, was pure and without shame. It was sin that corrupted their innocence and erected a stronghold of shame and guilt. Their nakedness was not news to God.

Note their response to God's next question. *"Have you eaten from the tree of which I commanded you that you should not eat?"* (Genesis 3:11). This is where we realize Adam was the first DJ. He defended and justified. Rather than taking responsibility, he responded,

The woman whom You gave to be with me, she gave me of the tree and I ate
(Genesis 3:12).

When God asked Eve, "What is this you have done?" *she* responded, *"The serpent* deceived me and I ate"(Genesis 3:13).

Blame, Blame, Blame

Adam blamed Eve and then blamed God for giving him Eve. Eve blamed the devil and the blame game continues to this day. For centuries, people have refused to take responsibility for their decisions and actions. Human nature always wants to defend and justify their faults. When they do this, they have no idea that they are feeding and reinforcing deadly strongholds in their lives.

I am always amazed that, even though we carry wounds and resist His hand of healing, God knows the worst about us, yet in His everlasting compassion He loves us still.

Fallen humanity has become so twisted, and our deception so pervasive, we need to ask God to reveal the insidious nature of Satan's lies in our lives. When we get to that place of total surrender and vulnerability, we must ask the Holy Spirit to expose our strongholds. Can you hear God asking you...

- Who told *you* that you were naked?
- Who told *you* that you were barren?
- Who told *you* that you were inferior?
- Who told *you* that you were unworthy?
- Who told *you* that you were a failure?
- Who told *you* that you can't?

- Who told *you* it's impossible?

Fig leaves will never accomplish what God alone can do. He not only *removed* their fig leaves, the Bible says *God covered them*.

For Adam and his wife the LORD *God made tunics of skin and clothed them*
(Genesis 3:21).

Adam and Eve's story is a picture of God's loving care and healing for those who are willing to take off the fig leaves, expose their wounds and allow His grace *to clothe them, cleanse them and cover them with His love.*

Hannah was determined to expose and exterminate the strongholds in her life. The Bible details key words for pulling down strongholds in 2 Corinthians.

For the weapons of our warfare are not carnal but mighty in God for pulling down strongholds (2 Corinthians 10:4).

The word *mighty* is derived from the Greek word *dunatos*. Δυνατός; powerful or capable, able, possible, strong.[5]

In its original meaning, *dunatos* denotes having power and being strong. In Acts 1:8 Jesus says, "You shall receive *power* when the Holy Spirit has come upon you." The Greek word for power is *dunamis*, δύναμις force; specifically miraculous power, from which we get our English word "dynamite." This miraculous power is God's divine dynamite.[6]

The Bible states our weapons of war to break down strongholds are not physical, but "mighty in God." We see in the Garden, God's powerful yet gentle hand of grace. He clothed Adam and Eve and at the same time pulled down the most invincible strongholds that imprisoned them.

- "Pulling down" in its original Greek meaning kathairesis/ Καθαίρεσις - denotes a demolition or destruction. Figuratively, it means extinction.[7]

This definition depicts a towering structure crumbling and being demolished and crushed into rubble. Even more, this Greek *word picture* goes on to describe the structure being demolished to the point of extinction. This is what God wants to do to the strongholds in our lives, *if* we give Him full access and complete control. He will pulverize them with His Holy Power!

Forgiveness Sets Us Free

No matter what we experienced that caused the offense, bitterness can never be justified. No matter what the affliction or how it got there, it must be released before God can fully heal a broken heart.

The spiritual force that opens the soul for the greatest accessibility to God is forgiveness. Forgiveness ignites His grace and opens the door of your heart for God to take full control and release His healing virtue.

I believe, in her supplication, Hannah instantaneously cried out in forgiveness. Only then could she receive God's healing power that released the roots and residue of bitterness that had infected her for years.

Forgiveness is the only antidote for a vengeful heart. "[Unforgiveness] is an acid that can do more harm to the vessel in which it is stored than anything on which it is being poured."[8]

Through forgiveness, we are able to loose, uproot and exterminate the stronghold of bitterness. *Bitterness* ties you to those who have wounded you, but *forgiveness* unites you with the One who was wounded for you. Jesus is our wounded Savior and by His stripes you are healed. Without a forgiving heart, the inevitable conflicts and encounters of life will constantly infect and inflame the wounds.

In Luke 17:3,4, Jesus taught His disciples: "Take heed to yourselves. If your brother sins against you, rebuke him; and if he repents, forgive him. And if he sins against you seven times in a day and seven times in a day returns to you, saying, 'I repent,' you shall forgive him."

Peter came to Him and said, 'Lord, how often shall my brother sin against me and I forgive him? Up to seven times?' Jesus said to him, 'I do not say to you, up to seven times, but up to seventy times seven' (Matthew 18:21, 22).

Isn't this an incredible amount of forgiveness? Can you imagine? That's 490 times per day, 20 times per hour, once every three minutes! What Jesus was saying to Peter is, "It's not about the numbers, it's about the heart. It is not about the *quantity* of words, but the *quality* of your forgiveness."

Understand this: Jesus may not have been speaking of 490 separate, new offenses. When you forgive someone, the enemy will keep coming back to you with accusations to reopen the wound. What you need to do is remind yourself that you have forgiven this person *every time* the memory comes back or when the offenses are repeated. The echo of the offense will be silenced as true forgiveness overrides its voice. When the enemy tries to remind you of the past, you just tell him you don't live there anymore!

Often people may say they forgive, but deep inside they are holding onto the offense because they still want revenge. D.L. Moody puts it like this, "Those who say they will forgive but can't forget simply bury the hatchet, but leave the handle out for immediate use."

I understand that for many with deep hurts, this is a very hard thing to do, especially when confronted with continuous attacks like the ones Hannah endured from Peninnah. It would have been so easy to blame everything on Peninnah and Elkanah and yield to a vengeful spirit. But Hannah did not.

She did not accept the lie of bitterness that deceives people into believing, "If my circumstances change, or the people around me change, then I will change." She knew that the pathway to the miracle was letting go of the offense and forgiving the offender. She had to seek forgiveness to cleanse her heart.

One Degree Makes All the Difference

Hannah was now in God's purifying fire. The process of being refined by the fire of God's anointing is described in the Book of Malachi.

He will sit as a refiner and a purifier of silver; He will purify the sons of Levi and purge them as gold and silver, that they may offer to the LORD an offering in righteousness (Malachi 3:3).

Specific temperatures are required to liquefy different metals. *Steel* melts at 1,400 degrees, *silver* at 1,763 degrees and *gold* at 1,850 degrees Fahrenheit. The intensity of Hannah's struggle required heaven's epic heat to melt the strongholds in *her* heart. What will it take to melt *your* strongholds buried deep within?

One degree makes all the difference. Think about it. Water at 211 degrees is just hot water, but at 212 degrees it boils and becomes steam. Just one degree of heat is the difference between hot water and the power of steam.

Do not stop at 211 degrees! How many times have we been one degree from our deliverance? Revelation without deliverance is *shelf-knowledge*, knowledge that becomes dormant. Unless we apply it, it will be of no use to us. For Hannah, the curtain of revelation was opened when she examined her heart and went into extreme prayer.

Hannah wasn't stopping at 211 degrees of revelation. She went beyond

212 degrees. Hannah's determination "boiled" and took her *full steam ahead* to her deliverance.

Will you allow the passionate fire of your faith to release the power of forgiveness in your life? One degree is the difference between a hot cup of tea and the steam that can turn a turbine to power a city.

- One degree separates the good from the great.
- One degree off-course can take you 1,000 miles away from your destination.
- One degree will freeze or thaw water.
- One millisecond can determine the winner of a race.

Prepared and Positioned for the Miracle

There is a lesson to be learned as we come to the most intense moment of Hannah's life. It provides a powerful insight into the preparation necessary for the birth of her miracle. Just as I shared, you cannot *seize your destiny* until you *see your destiny* by faith. Likewise, you cannot exterminate a stronghold until you *identify* it.

What we have in this moment of time is the climax of the divine process in Hannah's deliverance. As Hannah entered the temple, "she was in bitterness of soul" trembling in deep travail. She confessed "bitterness of soul" and that she had "held her complaint *until now*." This is evidence that she was prepared to forgive in this very moment as a prerequisite to receiving her healing. She had come to a place of total surrender, allowing herself to be emotionally stripped before the Lord.

Hannah's extreme prayer vigil was about to elevate her beyond her victimized soul. Her determined heart called on her Holy God with every convulsive sob. As she travailed, the strongholds of bitterness, misery and anguish were shaken and loosed to their foundation.

When Hannah cried out to Eli the priest, "I have *poured out* my soul before the Lord," her choice of words was no coincidence. There is no other expression in the Hebrew language that defines this moment more concisely than these two words, *poured out*. It must have been God who placed this precise expression upon the tongue of Hannah, as a promise to all those desperately seeking deliverance and their miracle.

The phrase *poured out* in Hebrew is a progressive word that describes an intense action. *Poured out* comes from the Hebrew word *shaphak,* which means to spew out, to spill forth liquid metal, to expend intensively, to cast, gush out and to shed blood.⁹ This is a vivid description of what deliverance is! Hannah's faith elevated her determination as she now entered the process of *shaphak*.

This definition of the Hebrew word *poured out* gives us a glimpse of what takes place in the spiritual realm when the power of God exterminates strongholds.

The Hebrew word picture of this act of deliverance is more of a *process* than a one-time *event*. It begins with the physical positioning of the vessel. Hannah was positioned when she entered the temple, collapsed before the Lord in extreme prayer and sprawled out prostrate before God. She laid her trembling heart, raw and naked before God at the altar. It was as though she was turning her soul inside out.

The spiritual process of deliverance accelerated, empowered by Hannah's prayer and trust in God. As Hannah's heart was fully opened, the strongholds that were imbedded in her mind, will and emotions were beginning to be uprooted and broken down under the power of God.

The word *shaphak* also denotes liquid metal. The liquefying metal symbolizes the spiritual process of deliverance when strongholds are pulverized and liquefied by the holy fire of God. The strongholds are melted by the intense passionate heat of God's holy anointing that is released through repentance and forgiveness. It was Hannah's fiery faith that fueled God's power of deliverance.

Shaphak also means "to expend intensively, to cast, gush out and spilled forth." This deliverance process describes a vessel that has released, rejected and expelled the contents that were once inside. This is the spiritual reality that takes place when the Word of God exterminates these strongholds, producing healed, healthy, fertile ground in the heart, ready to conceive God's vision.

Last, *shaphak* denotes shedding of blood. This describes the spiritual operation of God surgically removing our strongholds with skill and precision with the cutting-edge of His Word. It reminds me of an experience I had with one of my Teen Challenge students.

Back in the day, I would take the male students back-packing to the Catskill Mountains in upstate New York. Confronted with the elements, animals and sleeping on the rocky ground in little tents, it was an important part of their discipleship.

On one particular trip, I led 20 students on our annual survival training excursion. On the second day, we enjoyed the exhilaration of an intense, grueling climb. Later on that night, we set up camp and relaxed in the warmth of a roaring campfire. We concluded the night with prayer and fellowship, then bunked down under the stars on top of the mountain.

In the early morning, the quiet calm of the crisp mountain air was interrupted by piercing cries. Chris, a young student in his mid-twenties, awakened in his sleeping bag with a porcupine quill stuck in his back.

As we examined him, I chuckled a little and thought, "No big deal, I'll yank this thing out and we'll get on with the day."

To my surprise, when I attempted to remove the quill, it would not come out. As I pulled on it as hard as I could, his skin stretched out several inches from his body. I tugged the quill over and over and *still* it would not budge. By this time, the entire group had gathered and everyone was offering advice and solutions.

After calming everyone down, especially Chris, I realized the tip of the quill had tiny barbs that were embedded deep in his skin. Every time I pulled and let go, the quill dug deeper and deeper into his back.

Finally, I took a sharp hunting knife, pulled on the quill and stretched Chris' skin, as I cut into the flesh to release it. At first Chris cried out in pain, but when the quill finally popped out, with a heavy sigh of relief, he realized it was over. Even though Chris was bleeding, he was thankful to experience immediate peace.

The momentary pain of cutting into his skin ultimately released the barbs that were driving the quill deeper into his flesh. Untended, the quill could eventually have caused an infection and in some rare cases, death. Chris submitted to the pain of cutting it out because the pain of "staying the same" was worse than the "pain of removing the quill."

Removing the Barbs

Painful wounds run deep. People who have experienced abuse, disappointment or failure, whether brought on by themselves or inflicted by others, feel the pain of those wounds until they are treated and healed. From emotional and mental abuse, like Hannah endured, to sexual abuse, rape or incest, these wounds can paralyze the soul.

Rejection or betrayal by those that you love and trust, or the scars of divorce, can bury deep within the soul. Like a surgeon who must remove a cancerous tumor to heal a sick body, God at times, has to spiritually cut these strongholds of bitterness out, so that the soul can be clean and healthy.

Betrayal, abuse and rejection all have barbs of bitterness that can penetrate your memories and emotions. The quill is a clear example of a spiritual stronghold that must be removed or it will dig deeper and deeper into the soul.

Untended, these barbs begin to dig themselves in and eventually require *spiritual* surgery to remove them. When your healing and deliverance comes, your pain will subside and eventually the scars will become your testimony. Your pain will be forgotten. God will give you a song of deliverance that you will sing to the hearts of those who bear the same wounds.

When Hannah entered the operating room of the temple, she came fully surrendered with her heart open for God to perform surgery. Hannah not only unlocked and opened the door of her heart, she took the hinges off and removed the door completely, allowing God to fully access the deepest recesses of her soul. This was the pivotal moment of Hannah's deliverance. God was now able to pull down her strongholds and take Hannah's dreams into His healing embrace.

Ten Miraculous Days of Prayer

Like Hannah, my mother knew what it was like to face the impossible and believe God. With sheer determination, she picked herself up from the curb and struggled back into the house. Dragging her battered body up the stairs, she sensed a power greater than her own. She re-entered that dimly lit bedroom, closed the door and locked it behind her. She knew it was time to take action. In a personal, spiritual call to arms, she declared war on the devil.

That miraculous night, her bedroom became a divine operating room where her miracle began. It was more than Billy Graham's message of healing, it was God's presence. Her cry of deliverance was about to transform her sorrow into her song, as she knelt crying out to God.

My mother went from travail to supplication and surrendered everything to Jesus Christ. In that room, she did more than kick Valium and psychotropic drugs. She held on to the bedpost and cried out to God. No one in the family knew what was taking place except her and God. Later on, doctors told us that going cold turkey from the medications she was addicted to should have sent her into convulsions, seizures and possibly death from withdrawal.

But the power of God kept her.

For ten days, she tarried in that room. The sheets on her bed, soaked with sweat and tears, testified to her determination to break the strongholds of addiction and mental illness.

My mother poured out her soul to the Lord. She was experiencing *shaphak* the same way Hannah experienced it in the temple. Her strongholds were being rooted out, crushed and exterminated. She relentlessly prayed for deliverance and healing and God answered her prayers. Her miracle destiny was born.

On that tenth day, Mama Jack stepped out of that room in resurrection power. She was healed of mental illness, set free from her addictions and miraculously transformed by God. Like Hannah, even though the circumstances of her family had not changed, she had! She was now on a mission to save her entire household. Through my mother's powerful transformation, myself and over 40 members of my family received Christ and freedom from their addictions through the ministry of Teen Challenge.

Supernatural Power

Hannah, who had already examined her soul, knew that the strongholds could not be pulled down by carnal means. This purging and breaking process could only effectively occur through the holy fire of God's intervention in her life.

As Hannah poured out her soul to the Lord, God's anointing permeated this vessel of honor, breaking up the fallow ground and demolishing the strongholds of bitterness, misery, anguish and sorrow. The power of God, His Word and His holy promise crushed them into pieces as His blazing anointed fire exterminated the strongholds.

I can just see her breathe a sigh of relief, catching her breath with mixed emotions. While she carried herself with dignity, she was filled with grand expectations and peace in her spirit. Deliverance had come. Her soul was now free, full of faith and ready to expect her miracle.

EXPECT YOUR MIRACLE

So it came to pass in the process of time that Hannah conceived and bore a son and called his name Samuel, saying, 'Because I have asked for him from the LORD'
(1 Samuel 1:20).

As we look back on that Passover setting in verse 8, "Then Elkanah her husband said to her, 'Hannah, why do you weep? Why do you not eat? And why is your heart grieved?'"

I believe Hannah was fasting because she was focused on the will of God. Her obedience would lead to that defining moment as Hannah made her move of faith to the temple in verse 9.

So Hannah arose after they had finished eating and drinking in Shiloh
(1 Samuel 1:9).

I believe that prior to coming to the temple Hannah sensed in her heart that this was her time and this was her year. Keep in mind that year after year she had gone to the temple with her family only to be ridiculed and provoked by Peninnah. However, this year she determined *it would be different.*

This was Hannah's miracle year! It was her year of victory and her year for the vision to become a reality. This was Hannah's triumphal moment in time! By faith she arose and claimed, "This year is *my* year!"

Miracle on the Way

The amazing dynamic of Hannah's miracle is that although she had been marked, miserable, misunderstood and marred, **the miracle was still hers.** She knew her miracle was still in reach. She was no longer going to wait for her circumstances or the people in her life to change. She was not dependent on her husband or pastor's ability to understand her or believe in her vision. She trusted in God and resolved in her heart that unjust conditions were not going to define her life or detour her from her vision.

Hannah refused to be swayed by what the world said she could *not* do. Instead, she chose to embrace what God *would* do in her and through her. She had faith in the One who planted the vision in her heart. No matter what storm she faced, no matter how hard the wind blew or how strong the undercurrent, she would not give up.

The trumpet of change sounds with five words in 1 Samuel 1:20, **"In the process of time."**

These words are history-making, life-changing, transforming words of promise that herald Hannah's healing and miracle. God, who abides in eternity, has chosen to reveal His plans *in the process of time*.

In the Book of Ecclesiastes, God inspired Solomon to write, *"He has made everything beautiful in its time"* (Ecclesiastes 3:11).

The Bible states that the wisdom of Solomon surpassed all the kings of the earth. He penned this truth, filled with faith, hope and beauty. Solomon opens Ecclesiastes three by declaring:

To everything there is a season, a time for every purpose under heaven: A time to be born and a time to die; a time to plant and a time to pluck what is planted; A time to kill and a time to heal; a time to break down and a time to build up; A time to weep and a time to laugh; a time to mourn and a time to dance; A time to cast away stones and a time to gather stones; a time to embrace and a time to refrain from embracing; A time to gain and a time to lose; a time to keep and a time to throw away; A time to tear and a time to sew; a time to keep silence and a time to speak (Ecclesiastes 3:1-7).

There are seasons in life that prepare us for every situation we will face. We experience many trials in the journey; each trial is a season of growth. God carries us through as we embrace the greater things to come in our life mission. Hannah's rugged road now leads her to her richest blessing.

Seize the Moment

You may have already identified with Hannah's journey. Has the trial and suffering endured by Hannah drawn you into the chapters of her life?

Have you ever experienced the wounds of abuse and the pain of rejection and betrayal? Are you merely surviving each day with disappointment and dashed expectations? Are you really living life or just paying bills until you die?

Do you have a dream, a vision or destiny, conceived in your heart but feel paralyzed, boxed in and shackled? Are you fighting the feeling that you have no voice and no one understands you?

If you are, then Hannah's miracle testimony is a word for you. Universities around the world use the Latin expression, *carpe diem*, which means "seize the day." They encourage their students, graduates and faculty to take hold of their dreams and go after them. It's time for you to seize the moment!

This is Your Time!

Let me say to you with certainty, "This is *YOUR time and YOUR moment!* This is *YOUR year* and *YOUR miracle hour of destiny!* But remember, the battle is the Lord's! Surrender and release every snare, offense, wound, betrayal and stronghold! Receive the healing that Christ has provided for you on Calvary! The resurrection power of God is yours, so seize the moment. *Carpe diem!*"

Hannah refused to be trapped by the status quo. The literal Latin translation of status quo is *the state which you are in*. It is a term meaning the current or existing state of affairs or, as John Maxwell says, "the mess we're in." The problem with settling for *the state which you are in* is that you stay in your own *current* and miss out on God's *current*. The great danger is that you miss out on the opportunity to experience *how new and great things can be.*

Back in the day on the street, a common phrase of greeting was, "What's happening?"

The usual response was, "Same O, Same O!" Friends, God did not create us to *live* in the *status quo* of "Same O, Same O!" He created us to live in the creative landscape of vision that He has deposited in our hearts.

Because I Asked For Him

How many people have settled for second best, or just good enough, instead of seeking God for *His best?* God always wants the best for us. The Bible says, "You do not have because you do not ask" (James 4:2). In the temple, Hannah asked God for a child with expectant faith.

> *So it came to pass in the process of time, that Hannah conceived and bore a son and called his name Samuel, saying, 'Because I have asked for him from the LORD'*
> (1 Samuel 1:20).

Hannah's faith stands out above and beyond her strongholds. It was her faith that fueled her perseverance to petition God and believe that He would reward her and fill her womb. The Book of Hebrews declares:

> *Without faith it is impossible to please Him, for he who comes to God must believe that He is and that He is a rewarder of those who diligently seek Him*
> (Hebrews 11:6).

When Hannah asked God for a child, it pleased Him because she diligently *sought* God and believed her vision would come to pass.

In the Process of Time

This moment was Hannah's *pinnacle process of time*. The floodgates of heaven were about to open her womb for a miracle as God was ready to do a new thing.

Hannah's determined desire fires up *my* right brain visionary neurons. I relate it to a truth that was written 300 years after Hannah's story by the prophet Isaiah.

Do not remember the former things, nor consider the things of old. Behold, I will do a new thing, now it shall spring forth; shall you not know it? I will even make a road in the wilderness and rivers in the desert (Isaiah 43:18, 19).

This is a word of promise to all those who want to make a radical commitment to let God do a new thing in their lives. Are *you* tired of the "Same O, Same O" life of misery? If you are, this promise is for you.

No more wilderness or desert living! No more wilderness or desert thinking! No more wilderness or desert womb! What God is saying to all of us is, "Don't consider the *old*. Don't become content with the *old* wounded way. Don't settle for a dead end wilderness road that leads you to that *old* desert living, which keeps you doing the same *old* thing!"

Isaiah used the word "behold" to transition from the *old* way of living to God's *new* way of living.

Behold, I will do a new thing (Isaiah 43:19).

In the Bible, the word "behold" was used to announce a *royal decree* from the king to his people. The king's herald would come out to the city square and announce the royal proclamation.

Hannah heard the announcement of her miracle from the Holy Spirit. God's herald from heaven told her that *this* was her miracle moment! Go after the miracle, proclaim the miracle, seize the miracle and birth the miracle. Remember Isaiah's proclamation is God's royal declaration to everyone who desires for God to do a new thing in their lives.

Press In and Press On

For three decades I have worked with people battling life-controlling problems. The turning point of their transformation has often come when they realized that the pain of remaining the same was *greater* than the pain of change.

Don't assume that when you covenant with God for deep change that the attacks of the enemy will immediately cease. Often, the opposite happens. The attacks on your vision will increase. Although Peninnah's attacks continued, they did not detour Hannah's vision. Instead, they fueled a fire within Hannah's heart to go after her miracle with sheer determination.

Hannah refused to continue to endure the pain of staying the same. She seized the moment and stepped into a realm of faith that transformed her beaten-down mentality into a faith-filled attitude of vision, purpose and promise.

So Hannah arose after they had finished eating and drinking in Shiloh
(1 Samuel 1:9).

This expression, "so Hannah arose" is for all of us who run with vision, facing the stumbling blocks of life. Just as explosive and prophetic as the five words *"in the process of time"* are, so are the three words *"so Hannah arose!"*

The Hebrew word for "arose" is quwm- קום*; to rise, confirm, decree, endure, lift up, make new, establish, stir up, strengthen, succeed.*[1]

When Hannah arose from Passover dinner, the gate to her miracle was opened. Hannah entered the spiritual arena of the temple with fiery faith. This act of rising up describes Hannah's disposition inwardly and outwardly.

Inwardly, her spirit was stirred up by an abiding decree of faith. When she "arose," as in the Hebrew word, *quwm*, her action expressed a covenant decree – a no turning back commitment.

Outwardly, Hannah strengthened herself in the Lord and stood up with a spirit of determination. Her expression of faith confirmed the promise that she had held onto for so long. She may have been knocked down, but she was never knocked out! As Scripture tells us...

For a righteous man may fall seven times and rise again (Proverbs 24:16).

Deep in her soul, with sheer determination, her heart cried out, "It can't end like this!" Hannah's action was not just a religious routine, but an act of engagement in spiritual warfare. With expectant faith, she marched to the temple.

With that first step toward the temple, her faith was ignited and fueled by her belief that God was going to answer her prayer. What we see in Hannah's attitude is *the power of a made-up mind*.

She stepped into the spiritual jet stream of her destiny. This was her triumphal entry, the miracle moment in her saga. From barrenness to birthing her vision, the stage was set and the curtain was open. The facades were down as she took those steps to her promise. With each step, her resolve increased. Her miracle was at hand as she entered the temple.

Take Your Position

Despite Hannah's slumped silhouette, there was a divine power within. She had positioned herself in faith for the battle. The Bible declares,

The Lord will fight for you and you shall hold your peace (Exodus 14:14).

The battle is the LORD's! (1 Samuel 17:47).

For our weapons of warfare are not carnal but mighty in God...
(2 Corinthians 10:4).

This miraculous scene unfolded dramatically as Hannah's spirit erupted in deep travail. She poured out her soul to the Lord before the altar. As she trembled in God's holy presence, she locked into His throne room in supplication for her promised son. As Hannah emptied herself, the strongholds were loosed and her soul was flushed out as the presence of Almighty God filled her entire being.

And it happened, as she continued praying before the LORD, that Eli watched her mouth. Now Hannah spoke in her heart; only her lips moved, but her voice was not heard (1 Samuel 1:12, 13).

As Hannah, our gentle warrior, stepped out in faith, it was at this moment that her soul was fully delivered and healed. I can see her prostrate and exhausted on the temple floor, resting in God's loving care.

Eli, on the other hand, thought she was drunk. His harsh, degrading accusation struck her like a blow.

So Eli said to her, 'How long will you be drunk? Put your wine away from you!'

(1 Samuel 1:14).

Eli's assumption gives us some insight into how Hannah may have looked when she came into the temple. Perhaps she staggered as she entered, in deep travail and supplication, broken and bowed in spirit, falling to her knees under the burden of her soul.

But everything had now changed. The clearest evidence of supernatural grace was seen in her reverential response to Eli's harsh judgment.

It is obvious that she had been with the Lord. Her response was covered in faith by the promise she held in her heart. She lifted her head with the glow of God's presence radiating from her face and looked upon the dark, fleshly eyes of Eli and replied:

No, my lord, I am a woman of sorrowful spirit. I have drunk neither wine nor intoxicating drink, but have poured out my soul before the LORD. Do not consider your maidservant a wicked woman, for out of the abundance of my complaint and grief I have spoken until now (1 Samuel 1:15, 16).

Hannah held her complaint until this moment of time, which testifies of her godly, reverential discipline. She had the grace to hold back, knowing that the time was coming when she was going to let it all out. Hannah had a holy discontent that was about to erupt in her soul.

Her humble reply immediately transformed Eli's impression of her. Suddenly, he saw the shekinah glory illuminating Hannah's countenance as her holy response pierced his soul and spiritually sobered him. The fact that she was not a temple drunk crashed over his heart like a tidal wave, as he caught a fresh vision of this godly woman of miracles.

Answer To Prayer

I can imagine the look on Eli's face as this worn-out priest fell back under the power of God, his body shaken by the fear of the Lord. With the divine revelation that this woman had been touched by God's glory, he *knew* God had answered her prayer.

Did Eli know her prayer was for a child? I'm not sure, because there is no biblical reference. But, one thing I am sure of is that when he saw God's glory radiating from Hannah's face, he knew whatever she had asked of God, she got it.

Eli answered and said, 'Go in peace and the God of Israel grant your petition which you have asked of Him' (1 Samuel 1:17).

His words may have *confirmed* her miracle, but it was Hannah's faith that *conceived* it. Eli's ability to finally discern God's presence and favor was inspired by the humility of Hannah's response and the example of her unwavering faith.

And she said, "Let your maidservant find favor in your sight." So the woman went her way and ate and her face was no longer sad (1 Samuel 1:18).

Hannah's face shone with new life and hope. The joy of healing, peace and motherhood radiated from every pore of her being. Like a marathon runner, bursting across the finish line, lifting her hands in victory, Hannah knew the war was over and that the battle had been won. Her vision was conceived and about to be birthed.

Vision Revived

Hannah in a spiritual sense was reborn with new life, resurrected vision, and a greater passion for her mission.

Then they rose early in the morning and worshiped before the LORD and returned and came to their house at Ramah. And Elkanah knew Hannah his wife and the LORD remembered her (1 Samuel 1:19).

The trip back to the hill country of Ephraim was no longer drudgery. Hannah's dreaded encounters with relentless opposition were already a distant memory. She had a different walk and enjoyed a different talk. The joyous bounce was back in her step and her countenance was glowing with God's favor. An aura of faith, hope and love surrounded her. I am sure even Peninnah noticed this new stride from a distance.

Hannah confidently walked up to her husband, wrapped her arms around his neck. She gazed into his eyes with a romantic expectancy that he had not seen since those first wonderful years of their marriage. She excitedly whispered, "God has confirmed that I will bear you a son!"

Peninnah glared darkly at Hannah for her insolence. "How dare this useless, barren shell of a woman step in front of me and take hold of *my* husband. One month from now that useless Hannah will be sobbing in the background, disappointed once again!"

What Peninnah didn't know was that this *was* a *different* Hannah. The wounded, insecure woman, who once wondered if she would ever have a baby, was forever gone. Now a secure woman of faith, seasoned by life's trials, stood before her.

Hannah didn't even notice Peninnah. She had no time to waste trying to prove anything to her. Peninnah's vicious attacks were now a part of her past, thrown into the sea of forgiveness and buried in the ocean of forgetfulness. Hannah's life had been elevated by faith, determination and her miracle.

She now walked confidently by her husband's side and Peninnah is never mentioned again in the Bible. Her very existence falls off the pages of biblical history.

As Elkanah and Hannah journeyed back home, their love was renewed, their passion reignited. Their romance was restored and their dreams transformed.

The mountain country of Ephraim seemed brand new. The hills, intersected by wide plains and streams of running water, were alive with vegetation. The increasing beauty as they traveled north from Shiloh appeared to be more breathtaking. Every mountain they climbed was a joy; every step they took into the fertile valleys was a delight. The landscape seemed more lush with palm trees, as the fragrance of blooming flowers filled the air.

Finally, they arrived in the city of Ramah, in the land of the Ephraimites. Elkanah, with a pounding heart, swept Hannah into his arms and carried her over the threshold into their home once again. Like newlyweds with youthful excitement, they started their second honeymoon.

I believe that not only was Hannah's life transformed, but Elkanah's life was changed too. The years of seeing Hannah burdened with grief were gone. He rejoiced and his faith in God increased as he saw his beloved's sorrow turn to joy. Her discouragement had vanished. Her insecurities had disappeared. Not only that, but Elkanah began to *understand*. He finally got it! He was no longer satisfied to be *better than 10 sons* for his wife, but now desired to be part of *her vision*.

Never Forget! God Always Remembers!

And the LORD remembered her (1 Samuel 1:19).

God remembered Hannah. God remembered her pain, her suffering and her misery. Most of all, God remembered her prayer and covenant request. How profound is this verse to all of us who have a vision that seems impossible!

Never *forget* that God always *remembers*. Your need is always before Him *and* He remembers to forget your past failures. You will *never* be abandoned. You will never be alone. No matter what man may do, God will never forget His promise to you! Since the beginning, God has reminded us that He will remember His covenant with us.

Therefore know that the LORD your God, He is God, the faithful God who keeps covenant and mercy for a thousand generations with those who love Him and keep His commandments (Deuteronomy 7:9).

Let us hold fast the confession of our hope without wavering, for He who promised is faithful (Hebrews 10:23).

The Day Came!

The process of time had arrived. Was it six weeks? Two months? We don't know. But finally, Hannah's confirmation of Hannah's conception was revealed. I can imagine her excitement as she burst out of the house with uncontainable joy to share the good news with her beloved Elkanah.

"Honey!" Hannah exclaimed, "I'm pregnant! We're going to have a baby! God has answered our prayers!" With elation and tears of thanksgiving, their rejoicing echoed throughout the house and the report spread throughout the town.

So it came to pass in the process of time that Hannah conceived and bore a son and called his name Samuel, saying, 'Because I have asked for him from the LORD'
(1 Samuel 1:20).

Her Miracle Bestowed

Hannah experienced the fulfillment of her vision. Finally, that miraculous day came as she delivered her son. Even through her labor pains, she rejoiced at the manifestation of God's promise.

What an intensely painful, yet inspiring triumphal testimony to the world. I can only imagine the elation and celebration of God's grace and faithfulness that Hannah and Elkanah experienced when Samuel was born.

I can hear Hannah thanking God as she held God's gift. With tears of joy streaming down her cheeks, she snuggled her precious son close to her breast in loving embrace. Her miracle is born, her vision has come to pass and her destiny has set its course. Even the town busybodies were gathered around the house, amazed at God's miracle.

Then of course, there is the proud Papa! I see Elkanah taking his newborn boy, holding him up toward the heavens unto the Lord. With a heart bursting with joy, dedicating him to Almighty God, he celebrates the divine destiny and mission of this little baby.

Reason for the Miracle Season

What a miracle and what a journey. Hannah triumphed because she knew her fight was not against man. She did not have to convince Elkanah to listen, understand, support or honor her. Her fight was not with Peninnah, her family or society. It was not against her priest Eli, who carelessly called her a drunk.

Her fight was to guard her heart against the rulers of darkness and the spirit of bitterness, doubt and discouragement. Their mission was to destroy her faith and infiltrate her soul with defeat. Hannah *never* stopped believing in her vision and trusting in God.

It was her *faith* and *determination* that changed the course of her life. She poured out her soul to the Lord and allowed *Him* to change her inner being. This transformed her life, her family's destiny *and* even the nation of Israel. Her obedience *ultimately* changed the course of history. She positioned herself and God did the rest.

Never be afraid to stand up for what you believe. Remember, if you stand for nothing, you fall for anything. It's not easy to embrace and nurture a cause, especially when you're marked by society. But, as you trust in God and allow Him to guide you and fight your battle, your vision and mission will turn into your miracle destiny.

The final blessing of this story is that the miracle of Samuel's birth was not the end, but the start of a new season of fruitfulness. Hannah's past humiliation was transformed into her present celebration. After the birth of her miracle son, Samuel, Hannah brought him back to the temple and dedicated him to the service of the Lord. God rewarded her faithfulness and blessed her womb and multiplied her promise with five more children.

And the LORD visited Hannah, so that she conceived and bore three sons and two daughters. Meanwhile the child Samuel grew before the LORD (1 Samuel 2:21).

I don't know what your struggle is today, but I know that if God birthed a miracle in Hannah's life after years of being, mocked, marred, marked, miserable and misunderstood, *He can do it!* He can meet you right where you are. Hannah's journey and prayer is a reminder that even in your place of emptiness and despair, *God is always there for you.*

God turned Hannah's bitterness into beauty,
Her misery into a miracle,
Her pain into praise,
Her sorrow into a song,
and her tragedy to triumph.

The end of a thing is better than its beginning (Ecclesiastes 7:8).

And the best is yet to come.
If God did it for Hannah, He can do it for you.

Now to Him who is able to do exceedingly abundantly above all that we ask or think, according to the power that works in us, to Him be glory in the church by Christ Jesus to all generations, forever and ever. Amen (Ephesians 3:20).

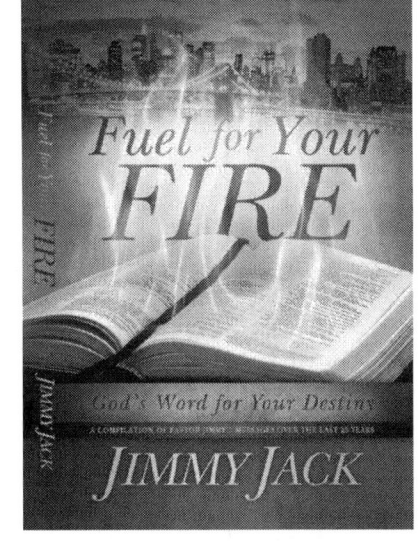

Also Available   Coming Soon

The Jimmy Jack Story is the life journey of the youngest of nine children set against the turbulent times of the sixties, seventies and eighties. His dad was committed into a psychiatric ward 3 times and his mom 5 times. With no parental guidance, Jimmy became a hopeless, homeless drug addict and alcoholic. However, that's not the end of the Jimmy Jack story. The title tells it all –*I Can Dream Again*.

Fuel for Your Fire is a power-packed book of dynamic messages written by Jimmy Jack. These teachings were birthed out of his heart and preached in the streets of New York City, International Crusades, Conferences and at his Church, Freedom Chapel International Worship Center. From "Gethsemane Experience" to "Maturing through Hard Times," "Passion for Your Purpose," "Desiring a Double Portion" and your "Supernatural Burning Destiny," these messages will inspire, ignite and influence you to walk deeper with God, while developing your leadership and servanthood skills!

If you would like to receive other resources, please call (631) 789-5050.

ENDNOTES

Chapter 1: Mission
1. Strong's Hebrew and Greek Dictionaries Edition: Third Copyright: Electronic Edition STEP Files Copyright 2003, Quick Verse, a division of Findex.com, Inc.

2. Sarah Young. *Jesus Lives.* (Nashville: Thomas Nelson, 2009), 52.

3. Rick Warren. *The Purpose Driven Life: What on Earth Am I Here For?* (Grand Rapids: Zondervan, 2012), 23.

4. Mark Batterson. *Wild Goose Chase: Reclaim the Adventure of Pursuing God.* (Colorado Springs: Multnomah, 2008), 38-39.

5. "Pinterest," accessed August 16th 2014, http://www.pinterest.com/lissie1342/faith-sees-the-invisible-believes-the-unbelievable/

6. John Blanchard, ed., *Gathered Gold: A Treasury of Quotations for Christians* George Muller. (Hertfordshire: Evangelical Press, 1984), 93.

Chapter 2: Marriage
1. Strong's Hebrew and Greek Dictionaries Edition: Third Copyright: Electronic Edition STEP Files Copyright 2003, Quick Verse, a division of Findex.com, Inc.

2. "Why Immerse in the Mikveh?" accessed February 5th 2013, http://www.myjewishlearning.com/life/Life_Events/Conversion/Conversion_Process/Mikveh.shtml

3. "The Seven Blessings Recited At A Traditional Jewish Wedding," accessed February 5th 2013, http://www.ou.org/wedding/7brachot.htm

4. "The Jewish Wedding Ceremony," accessed February 5th 2013, http://ohr.edu/1087

5. "The Seven Blessings Recited At A Traditional Jewish Wedding," accessed February 5th 2013, http://www.ou.org/wedding/7brachot.htm

Chapter 3: Marked

1. Rev. Bobby Lloyd, President of Long Island Citizens for Community Values

2. PC Study Bible Version 2.11, Biblesoft, February 1998, Seattle, WA, James Gilbertson.

Chapter 4: Miserable

1. PC Study Bible Version 2.11, Biblesoft, February 1998, Seattle, WA, James Gilbertson.

2. Ibid

3. Ibid

4. "Disaster, Rescue and Recover," accessed February 5th 2013, http://www.lusitania.net/disaster.htm

5. "The Sinking of the Lusitania," accessed February 5th 2013, http://www.eyewitnesstohistory.com/snpwwi2.htm

6. "A Deadly Cargo and the Falsified Manifests," accessed February 5th 2013, http://www.lusitania.net/deadlycargo.htm

Chapter 5: Misunderstood

1. Journal of Human Reproductive Sciences Publisher: Indian Society of Assisted Reproduction, Medknow Publications, PVT. Ltd. Description ISSN 0974-1208 OCLC, 225867673. Material type Periodical, Internet resource.

2. Mark Batterson. *The Circle Maker: Praying Circles Around Your Biggest Dreams and Greatest Fears.* (Austin: Zondervan, 2011), 75-76.

3. "Maslow's Hierarchy of Needs," accessed February 5th 2013, http://www.comprofessor.com/2010/04/maslows-hierarchy-of-needs.html

Chapter 6: Marred

1. PC Study Bible Version 2.11, Biblesoft, February 1998, Seattle, WA, James Gilbertson.

2. Ibid

3. "The Declaration of Independence," accessed February 5th 2013, http://www.ushistory.org/declaration/document/

END NOTES

4. "Pinterest," accessed August 16th 2014, http://www.pinterest.com/hannasherrie/rick-warren/

Chapter 7: Examine Soul

1. "Wilhelm Röntgen," accessed February 5th 2013, http://en.wikipedia.org/wiki/Wilhelm_R%C3%B6ntgen

2. PC Study Bible Version 2.11, Biblesoft, February 1998, Seattle, WA, James Gilbertson.

Chapter 7: Extreme Prayer

1. Oz Hillman, "Place of Nothingness," *Marketplace Leaders* (2013): 115.

2. "William P Young Quotes," accessed February 5th 2013, http://www.goodreads.com/quotes/102103-don-t-ever-discount-the-wonder-of-your-tears-they-can

Chapter 7: Exterminate the Strongholds

1. PC Study Bible Version 2.11, Biblesoft, February 1998, Seattle, WA, James Gilbertson.

2. Rick Renner. *Sparkling Gems from the Greek: 365 Greek Word Studies for Every Day of the Year To Sharpen Your Understanding of God's Word.* (Tulsa: Teach All Nations, 2003), 918.

3. "Vengeance Quotes," accessed February 5th 2013, http://thinkexist.com/quotes/with/keyword/vengeance/

4. "Forgiveness Quotes," accessed February 5th 2013, http://www.2prophetu.com/templates/_2prophetu2/details.asp?id=35585&PG=resources&CID=22987

5. Strong's Hebrew and Greek Dictionaries Edition: Third Copyright: Electronic Edition STEP Files Copyright 2003, Quick Verse, a division of Findex.com, Inc.

6. Ibid

7. Ibid

8. "Brainy Quote," Mark Twain, accessed September 16, 2014, http://www.brainyquote.com/quotes/quotes/m/marktwain120156.html

9. Strong'sHebrewandGreekDictionariesEdition:ThirdCopyright:Electronic EditionSTEPFilesCopyright2003,QuickVerse,adivisionofFindex.com,Inc.

Chapter 7: Expect Your Miracle

1. Strong's Hebrew and Greek Dictionaries Edition: Third Copyright: Electronic Edition STEP Files Copyright 2003, Quick Verse, a division of Findex.com, Inc.

We pray that this book has been a blessing to you. If it has, please let us know. If you would like a copy to send to a friend or need additional resources, please contact us at:

Jimmy Jack Ministries
641 Broadway
Amityville, NY 11701
Phone: (631) 789-5050

E-mail: Info@jimmyjackministries.org
Websites: http://www.litcny.org
http://www.rocktheblock.org
http://www.freedomchapelny.org
http://www.jimmyjackstory.com

Twitter: @jimmyjackny
Facebook: Jimmyjackministries

Copies are available above or online through Amazon, eBay and www.jimmyjackny.org.

If you or someone you love are in need of help, Please call Long Island Teen Challenge at 631-321-7070 or e-mail info@litcny.org.

There is a miracle waiting for you.
You can dream again!

Made in the USA
Columbia, SC
28 April 2018